Christian Light Education
Reading to Learn Series

Helping Hands

Second Grade Reader
Book 1

Compiled by Ruth K. Hobbs

Editorial Committee:
Ben Bergen
Keith E. Crider
James Hershberger
Sadie Schrock

CHRISTIAN LIGHT EDUCATION

A division of Christian Light Publications Inc.
Harrisonburg, Virginia 22801-1212

Christian Light Education, a division of
Christian Light Publications, Inc., Harrisonburg, VA 22801
© 1998 by Christian Light Publications, Inc.
All rights reserved. Published 1998
Printed in the United States of America

07 06 05 04 03 02 01 00 99 98   5 4 3 2 1

ISBN: 0-87813-933-8

Table of Contents

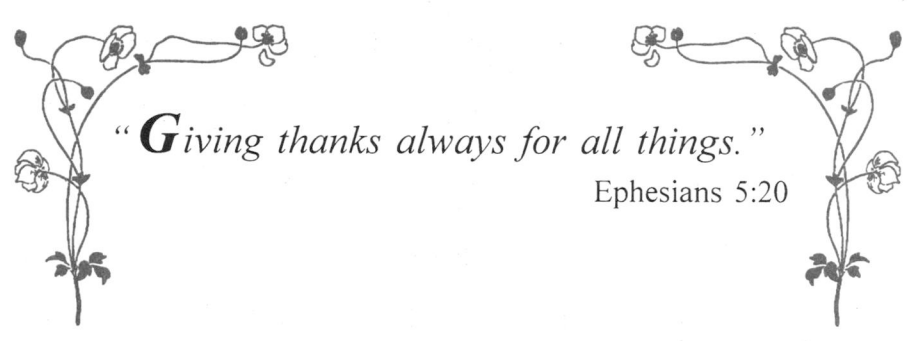

Nell's Dried Onions

Why did Grandma send dried onions to Nell?

"Here is a box for Miss Nell Freed," said Father, coming into the house.

"Oh, Father," cried Nell. "A box for me! Who is it from? What can it be?"

Father looked at the box. "It is from Grandma," he said. "You will have to open it to find out what is in it."

"Come, Mother," cried Nell. "Come and see what I got in the mail!"

Mother came and looked at the box. "Yes, it is from Grandma," she said.

"If it is from Grandma, I know it will be something nice," said Nell. "Maybe something good like candy. Maybe something **beautiful** like a doll."

But there was no candy or doll in the box. There was nothing but six brown things like balls.

"**Dried**-up **onions**!" cried Nell. "Why did Grandma send me onions? I don't even like onions. I thought it would be something nice. These are not good or beautiful. I will **throw** them away."

2

"I would not do that," said Father.

"No, don't do that," said Mother. "Just throw them in the onion box in the **pantry**. I'm sure Grandma had some good reason for sending them to you."

"All right," said Nell. "I don't want them. But what can I tell Grandma? I can't say I didn't like what she sent me. How can I **write** a **thank**-you note if I am not thankful?"

"How about waiting a little while before you write a thank-you note," said Mother.

"All right. Then maybe I can **think** of something to say."

Nell put the onions in the pantry and went out to play.

Nell did not see her mother take the six dried onions from the pantry. She

3

did not see her put them deep down in six **flower** pots in the **cellar**. She did not see her mother **water** the flower pots. In fact, Nell forgot all about the dried onions from Grandma until two or three weeks later.

Then one day she cried, "Oh, Mother, I just thought about what Grandma sent. I have not written a thank-you note to her. I still cannot think why she sent me dried onions. How can I be thankful for them?"

"Come with me to the cellar," said Mother. "Come and see what I did with the onions you did not want."

There in the cellar were the six flower pots. Nell saw the thick green tip of a plant poking up in each one.

"Oh, Mother, what are they? I

thought they were onions. Now I know they are not onions. They are some kind of flower. May we take them out of the cellar? Then I can watch them grow. May I water them?"

"Yes," said Mother. "They are flowers. They are **hyacinths**. You may water them. Hyacinths are beautiful flowers."

They put the six flower pots on the sunny sill of the dining room window. Nell gave them a little water every day.

Before long the windowsill was filled with beautiful pink and white and purple hyacinths. How sweet they smelled! Everyone said they were beautiful.

"I am thankful you did not throw them away. Now I can write a really *thankful* thank-you letter to Grandma,"

said Nell. "I wish she could see this beautiful windowsill. Won't she laugh when I tell her I thought the hyacinths she sent me were dried onions!"

6

If Nell had smelled Grandma's gift, she would not have thought it was onions.

Wonderful Smells

The world is full of wonderful smells,
And you have a nose that always tells
Of bread in the oven, hot and nice,
Of cake being baked with lots of spice,
Of a barn with fresh-cut hay in the
    mows,
Of horses and pigs and cats and cows,
Of a dog when he's warm and lies in
    the sun,
Of applesauce and chocolate and a sugar
    bun.
Wouldn't it be dreadful if you'd no nose
    to tell
Of every wonderful, wonderful smell?

–Zhenya Gay

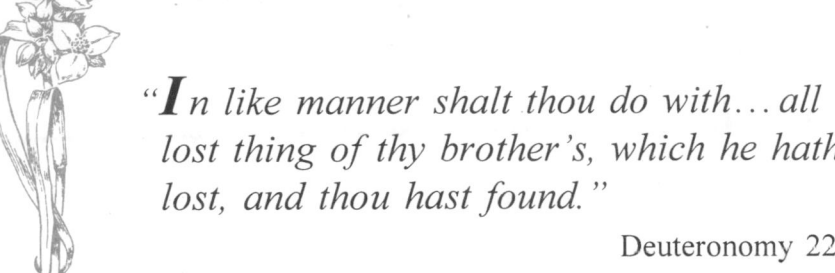

"In like manner shalt thou do with... all lost thing of thy brother's, which he hath lost, and thou hast found."

Deuteronomy 22:3

Johnny and the Blue Marble

Why didn't Johnny want the blue marble at the end of the story?

"Mother, what **verse** in the Bible would be a good one for me to learn?" asked Johnny one afternoon.

"**'Thou** God **seest** me' is a very good one," said Mother.

"What do 'thou' and 'seest' **mean**?" asked Johnny.

"They are Bible words that we don't often use," answered Mother. "They mean, 'God, You see me.'

"God keeps His eye on little boys and takes care of them. He also sees when they do something **wrong**. Little people, and big ones too, sometimes do things that are wrong when they think no one will know it."

"They **should** remember 'Thou God seest me,' shouldn't they?" said Johnny. "Then they would not do wrong things."

"Yes," answered Mother. "That is why the verse is a good one for you and me."

"I wish God could **speak** as well as He can see. But He can't, can He, Mother?"

"Oh, yes, He can," answered Mother quickly.

Johnny opened his eyes wide. "Can He? I never heard Him."

"You can't hear God's voice the same way you hear mine, but He can speak in two ways," said Mother.

"What does He sound like? Like the wind?" asked Johnny.

"No, God's voice does not sound like the wind. One way He speaks is in the Bible. When you read, 'Be ye kind,' that is God speaking to you.

"The other way is in a still small voice in your heart. Sometimes God makes you think of things He wants you to do or not do. That is His voice speaking to you."

"What does His voice say?"

"When you do something good, He says, 'That is right. That is right, My child.' When you want to do wrong, He says, 'Don't do that, Johnny. You should not do that, My child.'"

"I am going to **listen** for His voice," said Johnny. "I want to see if I can hear Him."

The rest of the afternoon and the next day, Johnny listened for the small voice. He seemed very happy, so he must have heard it saying, "That is right, My child."

One day when he took his **marbles** from his marble sack, out came a pretty blue one.

"What a pretty blue marble!" said his mother,

as she took it from his hand. "Where did you get it?"

Johnny did not **answer**. He quickly held out his hand for the blue marble; but Mother did not give it to him.

She looked at Johnny, but he did not look at her. He did not speak, but quickly put the other marbles into his pocket.

"Johnny, where did you get this marble? Does it belong to you?"

But Johnny did not answer.

"I guess I must keep this marble until you can tell me where you got it," said Mother, putting it into her pocket.

That night after family worship Mother and Daddy and Johnny were in the living room. Johnny climbed into Mother's lap. He laid his head on her

shoulder. He said in a low, sorry tone, "I took that marble, Mother."

"Took it!" said Mother. "Who did you take it from?"

"I took it from the ground at **school** today," said Johnny.

Then Daddy, who had been listening, asked, "Did it belong to the ground? How did the ground get it? Did the ground go to the store and buy it?"

"Buy it?" said Johnny. He tried to laugh at such a funny idea, but he could not even smile. He had heard that still small voice speaking all afternoon saying, "No, Johnny, no. You should not keep that marble. It is not yours. It belongs to some other boy. It is wrong for you to keep it."

But Johnny wanted the pretty blue marble. He did not want to listen to what the voice was saying.

Then Mother asked, "Whose marble is it? Some boy had it before it was on the ground. He lost it. Do you know who it belongs to?"

"Fred Mast, I guess," answered Johnny. "He used to have one like it, I think. But I found it on the ground. It would still be lost if I had not found it. Fred would not have it anyway."

"That is true," said Mother. "But you found it, so now it is not lost. It was all right to pick it up when you saw it. It was all right to put it into your pocket.

"But when you put it into your pocket, meaning to keep it, that was wrong.

"Did you not hear that still small voice speak? Didn't you hear it saying, 'No, Johnny, don't. It is not your

14

marble. You know it belongs to Fred Mast. You should not keep it.' Didn't you think of 'Thou God, seest me'?"

"No, Mother, I didn't hear any voice. I just quickly picked it up and put it into my pocket. It was so pretty. I don't have a blue one, and you can't buy that kind anymore." Johnny put his arms around his mother's neck. He began to cry.

Mother held him close.

Then Daddy said, "Did the blue marble make you happy? Would you be happy if we let you keep it? Would you like to take it to school and show the boys the blue marble you found?"

Johnny shook his head. He wiped his eyes. Then Mother took the blue marble from her pocket, and she gave it to him.

"I guess you forgot that God saw the

blue marble in your pocket today.
Maybe you forgot 'Thou God, seest me.'
Maybe you forgot God saw that you
wanted to keep the marble. That is
what made you so unhappy even when
you had the blue marble, isn't it?"

Johnny nodded. Then he smiled and said, "If God could see all that, then He can see what I plan to do with this blue marble when I get to school tomorrow."

The next morning, Johnny handed the blue marble to Fred Mast. He said, "I found it on the ground, but it is not mine. Isn't it yours, Fred?"

"Oh, Johnny. Thank you. I thought I had lost it for good. Uncle George gave it to me when I was little. He is dead now. It is the only thing I have to remember him by. Oh, I am so glad you found it."

As Johnny ran home he felt very happy, for he heard the voice speak in his heart, saying, "That is right. That is right, My child."

Abe and His Dog

Do you think the dog would have come
across the river if Abe had left him?

Once there was a boy named
Abraham Lincoln. His family called
him Abe.

He lived long ago with his father, mother, and baby sister in a **cabin** on a little farm. The cabin had only one room.

Abe and his family were very poor. It was hard for his father to make a living. There were rabbits and **squirrels** and bears and fish to eat. But things did not grow well on their little farm.

One day his father said to Abe, "Mother and I have sold this farm. The land is too poor. We have bought better land far away from here. We must **leave** and move to that place where the land is better. There we can grow the things we need. We must have more than rabbits and squirrels to eat."

In those days there were no trains or trucks. People had to move from place to place in a **wagon**. The wagon was

covered to keep things dry. The family could ride and sleep in the wagon.

So Abe's family put their things into a covered wagon. They had to leave everything they could not get into the wagon. They had two **strong oxen** to pull it.

It was near the end of winter. The roads were deep in mud.

Often the **heavy** wagon sank almost to the hubs of the wheels. But the oxen were strong. Slowly they kept walking. Slowly they would pull the heavy wagon out of the mud and keep going.

They went through woods full of rabbits and squirrels. They went up and down the hills. On and on they went toward the new cabin on the new farm.

In those days there were no bridges over the **rivers**. Abe's father had to find a place where the water was not too deep. Then he and Abe would get into the covered wagon with Mother and the baby. The strong oxen would slowly pull them across the river.

At that time of year some of the rivers had ice on them. It was thin ice and the oxen broke through at every step.

It was a long, cold trip. Often Abe and his father would **shiver** as they walked along. How glad they would all be to reach the little cabin on the new land. They knew it would be only a cabin with one room like the one they had to leave. But it would be home.

Abe and his father walked along by the wagon so the load would not be so heavy for the oxen. The only time they rode was when they had to cross a river.

Abe liked to pat the strong oxen as they slowly walked along. By his side ran his little dog. The dog seemed to like the trip, even though he, too, had to shiver sometimes. He liked to **bark** at the squirrels and send them flying up a tree. He liked to bark at rabbits and to run after them into the woods. The trip was all fun for him.

One day the little dog chased a rabbit far off into the woods until Abe could not hear him barking anymore. While he was gone the oxen came to a river. Abe and his father got into the covered wagon and the strong oxen pulled it across. They broke the ice at every step.

At last the oxen pulled the wagon up the bank on the other side. Abe and his father got out and began walking again.

They had gone on a little way when they heard barking behind them. Looking back, they saw Abe's little dog. He was running up and down the far bank of the river they had just crossed.

Abe ran back and tried to **coax** the dog to cross on the ice where the oxen had not broken it. But the little dog was too frightened. Abe could not coax him to leave the bank and cross the ice.

He could not coax him even to try.

"We shall have to leave him, if you can't coax him to come over," said Father. "The oxen cannot turn around in this deep mud."

"We can't leave him!" cried Abe. "He will freeze or starve! Hear how he cries for us!"

"I am sorry, Abe, but there is no way we can go back," said Father. "He could swim over if he would. The water is not deep at all."

"Then may I go over and get him?" asked Abe. "I cannot leave him."

"Yes, but don't waste any time. We will keep moving," Father replied.

Abe quickly pulled off his heavy shoes and socks. Then he rolled up his pants legs. Oh, how he shivered as he waded through the icy water to the other bank.

The happy little dog jumped all over Abe. Picking up the shivering little animal, the boy waded through the river again.

Abe pulled his socks and shoes onto his icy feet. He and his little dog soon caught up with the slow oxen.

All the rest of the trip until they came to the new cabin on the new land, the little dog did not leave the boy's side. He did not chase any more squirrels. He did not chase any more rabbits. He knew that the safest place for a little dog was there beside Abe.

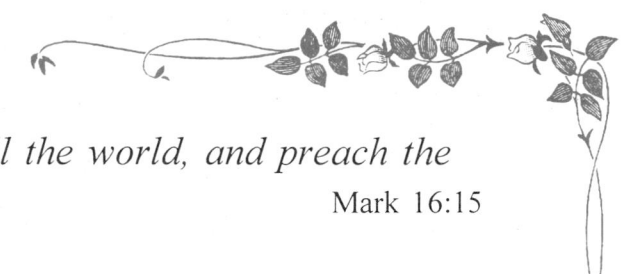

*"**G**o ye into all the world, and preach the gospel."*

Mark 16:15

The Bag of Birthday Bones

Part 1

Would you like to live where the sun shines all night?

"How old are you?" asked Missionary John.

Hands shot up all over the **schoolroom**.

"I'm six," said Tony.

"I'm **seven**," said Sue.

27

"I'm **eight**," said Ray.

"How do you know?" asked the missionary.

"Daddy says I am six," said Tony.

"Mother tells me I'm seven," said Sue.

"I've known how old I was since I was little," said Ray.

"How do your father and mother know? Do they count the days since you were **born**?"

All the boys and girls shook their heads. The schoolroom was quiet. No one said anything for a while.

Then Tony said, "My name is in the front of our big Bible. It says there when I was born."

Sue said, "We have a paper that the doctor gave when I was born. It says on

there what day my birthday is. That is
how I know."

"That is a birth **certificate**," said
Missionary John. "All of you have birth
certificates."

Ray said, "If we look on the **calendar** we can tell when our birthday comes. Then we are one year older."

Missionary John smiled. "All of you are right. But what if you had no Bible? What if you had no birth certificate? What if you had no calendar? Then how could you tell how old you were?"

Again the schoolroom was quiet. No hands went up. The children did not know.

"You know I am a missionary. I tell the story of Jesus to Eskimos. These Eskimos live in a **country** in the far north. They live near the top of the **world** in Greenland. Eskimos wear fur clothes. They do not live in the same kinds of houses that we do. They do not eat the same kind of food that we do.

"In that part of the country, summer

days are much longer than ours. The sun does not go down at all for **months**. It is light all night."

"Light all night!" cried the children.

"Yes, light all night," said Missionary John. "And winter nights are much longer than ours. The Eskimos do not see the sun at all for months. It is dark all day."

"Dark all day!" cried the children.

"Yes, dark all day. The sun stays below the **edge** of the world week after week. The Eskimos have no calendars. They cannot tell how many days have gone by."

Sue put up her hand. "Since they cannot count the days, how do they know when a year has gone by?" she asked.

"They have a way to tell," said Missionary John. "Even when they cannot count days on a calendar. They have a way of knowing when **spring** is coming.

"Many weeks of darkness pass. Then comes a time when the sky is lighter in the morning. Day after day the sky gets lighter and stays light longer. The Eskimos do not see the sun yet. But they know it is there below the edge of the world.

"Then one morning the bright rim of the sun peeps up for just a few minutes. Then it goes down again. But it is a time of great joy. 'The sun! The sun,' shout the children happily.

"The next day the sun rises a little higher. It stays up a little longer. The next day it rises higher yet. It stays up

a little longer yet. Then the Eskimos
know that winter is over and spring is
coming."

When you are pretending, you can play Eskimo even in the summer.

Let's Play Eskimo

Icicles glitter and the snowflakes fly.
Let's play Eskimo, you and I.

Build a little snow hut, wee, wee, wee.
Pat-a-cake it down so carefully.

Hollow out a door that we both crawl
  through,
Squatting on the floor as the North
  folk do.

Hitch a tiny dog to a sled, sled, sled.
Riding in the starlight when the sun
  has fled.

Little tallow candle, light it bright,
Winking with its eye in the still,
  dark night.

Play that our sandwiches are chunks
    of seal,

Frozen fish and sea bird eggs will be
    our meal.

And we know our coats of fur will keep
    us warm,

Just as God our Father will keep us
    safe from harm.

—Author unknown

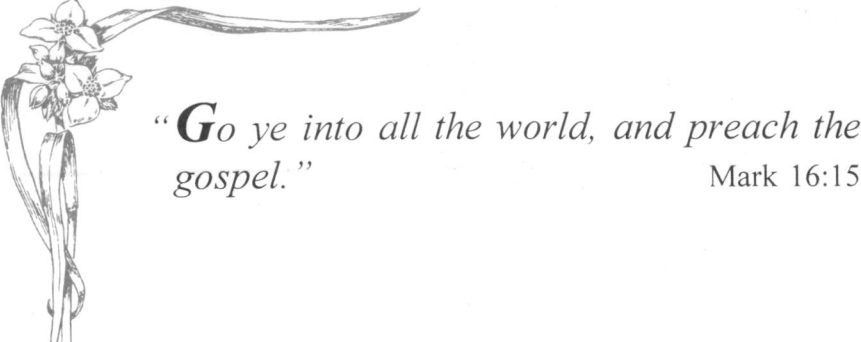

"Go ye into all the world, and preach the gospel."

Mark 16:15

The Bag of Birthday Bones

Part 2

Would you like to live where it is dark all day long?

"Since they don't have a calendar, how do they know when they have a birthday?" asked Tony.

"They don't know when their birthday is, but they do know how old they are," said Missionary John.

36

"How can they?" asked Sue.

"It's this way. When an Eskimo baby is born, its mother makes a small fur bag for its very own. At the end of the long winter night when the sun first peeps over the edge of the world, Mother puts a small bone in the fur bag.

"The next year when the sun again shows its bright edge for the first time, she puts another small bone in the birthday bag.

"Every year, on the day of the first sun, Eskimo mothers put another small bone in the little fur bags of all their children. If an Eskimo child forgets how old he is, he counts the bones in his birthday bag, and that tells him.

"Of course, the day of the first sun is not the child's real birthday. But it is the day he knows he is a year older because he gets a new bone in his birthday bag."

"I would rather have a birthday bag than a birth certificate," said Tony.

"So would I," said the other children.

"Maybe your teacher would help you make birthday bags out of some kind of fur," said Missionary John.

"Yes, I will," said the teacher, "but where will we get the bones?"

Hands went up all over the schoolroom. The teacher called on Ray.

"We could use little stones instead of bones," he said. "We could put a new stone in the bag on our birthdays."

"Yes, let's do it," cried the children.

"I will soon be going back to the country of Greenland," said Missionary John. "Will you pray for me as I teach the Eskimos about Jesus?"

"Yes, we will. Every time one of us puts a new stone in his birthday bag, we will remember to pray for you," said the children as they waved good-bye.

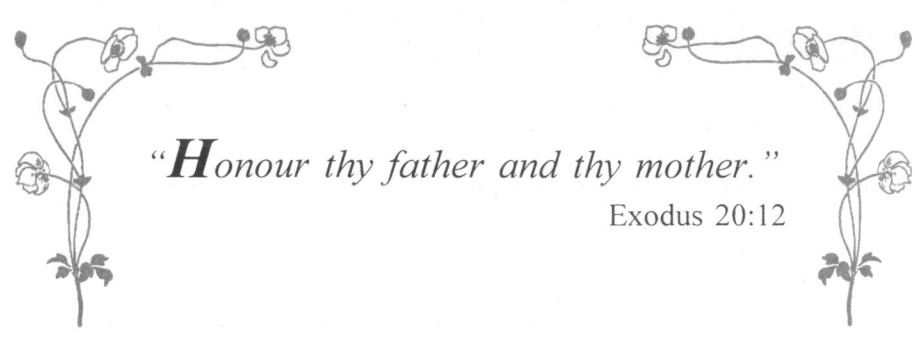

*"**H**onour thy father and thy mother."*

Exodus 20:12

Mr. Doodleburger Comes to Work

When did Mr. Doodleburger turn into Andy Lee?

Knock! Knock! Knock!

Mother stopped baking **cookies**. She went to the door. There stood her little boy.

"Well, hello, Andy Lee. Come on in. Why did you knock? **Couldn't** you open the door?"

"Hello, Mrs. White," said Andy Lee in a deep, big-man voice. "My name is **Mr.** Doodleburger. I am looking for a job. Do you have any work for me?"

"Oh, I see, Mr. Doodleburger," said Mother. "I am so glad you came. My day is very full. I do need some help. Now, let's see. What kind of work can you do?"

"Well, I know how to **carry** wood. I have **carried** a lot of wood in my life," said Andy Lee in his deep, big-man voice. He **squeezed** his lips shut to keep from laughing.

"Fine!" said Mother. "I am glad you can carry wood. I do need wood in my **woodbox**."

"Just tell me where your woodpile is, **Ma'am**."

"It is in the backyard. Come to the

window here and I will show
you. See it out there
between the fence and
the shed? You can
bring the wood in
the back door and
put it into the woodbox
here between the
cupboard and the stove."

"All right, Mrs. White."
Mr. Doodleburger went out
and got to work.

Before Mother had taken the last pan
of cookies out of the stove, the woodbox
was full. It was piled high.

"Now, what next, Mrs. White?" asked
Mr. Doodleburger.

"Well, I have been making cookies, as
you see. I would like to know if they are
good. Would you eat one or two and tell

me if you think they are all right? You may sit there on the **chair** and rest a bit while you eat."

"I will be glad to do that for you, Ma'am." Mr. Doodleburger took a soft, fat cookie and ate it.

"M-m-m-m. You do bake very good cookies, Mrs. White. I believe they are all right. Thank you so much." Mr. Doodleburger got off the chair. "Do you have any more work for me?"

"Yes, I do," answered Mother. "I have a little boy. His name is Andy Lee. He went outside a little while ago, but he forgot to pick up his toys before he left. Do you know how to pick up toys, Mr. Doodleburger?"

"Yes, I do, but I believe your little boy should have **picked** them up before he left."

"Well, he just forgets sometimes," said Mother.

"This job will not take me long," said Mr. Doodleburger. "Where do you want me to put them, Ma'am?"

"Just carry them to that blue toy box."

Mother washed the cookie pans and put them into the cupboard. By that time there was not a toy in sight. The blue toy box was full, and the lid was down.

"Say, Mr. Doodleburger! You are a good, fast worker! Couldn't you stay for supper? Mr. White will be home from work soon. Supper is on the stove. We would be glad to have you stay."

"Thank you, Ma'am. I believe I could do that," said Mr. Doodleburger. "Would you like me to set the table for you?"

"Yes, I would be happy to have you

do that. The dishes are in that cupboard. You can carry a plate of these cookies to the table, too."

By the time the table was set, the door opened and there was Daddy.

"Hello, Mother. Hello, Andy Lee. Any kisses for a working man tonight?"

Mother had one for him. Then she said quickly, "Mr. White, I would like you to meet Mr. Doodleburger. He came to work for us. He is going to stay for supper."

"Oh, hello, Mr. Doodleburger," said Daddy. "I am glad you came to help us." Then Daddy shook hands. Again Andy Lee squeezed his lips shut to keep from laughing.

"You may sit here between us," said Mother. "It is our little boy's chair, but I believe it will fit you."

"Thank you, Ma'am," said Andy Lee as he got onto the chair. "I believe it will!"

After the dishes were done and in the cupboard, Daddy said, "Mr. Doodleburger, couldn't you sleep here tonight? Couldn't you stay with us until our own boy comes back? I think you would fit in his bed all right."

"I believe I could do that, if you think his bed would really fit me. Thank you, Sir," said Mr. Doodleburger.

"Before we go to bed we like to read the Bible," said Daddy. "Will you have a chair?"

Mother and Daddy sat on the sofa. Mr. Doodleburger sat in the big chair. He sat very quietly until Daddy stopped reading.

Suddenly he jumped off the chair. He ran to the sofa. He squeezed in between

Mother and Daddy. He looked up at them.

"I don't want to be Mr. Doodleburger anymore. I want to be your own Andy Lee again. Now please read me a Bible story."

Mother put her arm around Andy Lee on one side. Daddy put his arm around him on the other side. They both squeezed him so tightly he had to laugh.

"I am so glad to have my own boy back again," said Daddy.

"So am I," said Mother. "I believe he is just as good a helper as Mr. Doodleburger was."

Daddy read Andy Lee a Bible story. Then he prayed, "Thank You, God, for Andy Lee. Thank You that he is such a good helper."

And Andy Lee prayed, "Thank You, that I am not really Mr. Doodleburger, but have my own mother and daddy."

Then he gave Mother and Daddy a tight squeeze and a hard kiss and ran off to his own bed. It fit just right.

Andy Lee played he was a grown-up man. It was fun for a while. But then he was glad to be himself again.

In this poem, someone is thinking how it would be if she were a worm.

Can you think of some things that would not be fun or nice if you were a worm?

I'd Like to Be a Worm

I'd like to be a worm
And squirm
In nice soft dirt,
And not have to worry
Or ever be sorry
Of getting mud on my nice
    clean shirt.

–Zhenya Gay

*"**F**ear thou not; for I am with thee."*

Isaiah 41:10

Emmy and
the Big Black Dog

Who was different at the end of the story,
Emmy or King?

It was not far to Bylers' farm and the **milk can** was small. Emmy was not thinking about that. She was thinking about King, the big black dog that always came out barking when Mother **drove** in for milk.

This was the first time Emmy was

going for milk **alone**. Before this, Mother got the milk on the way home from taking the children to school.

Now school was out and Mother said Emmy was big enough to walk to Bylers for the milk.

"I hope King will be **penned** in the **yard**," she said to herself. "What if he comes running out the lane at me!"

Bow-wow! Bow-wow!

Emmy's heart gave a great **leap**. It began to go **pound**-pound-pound-pound. *Oh, there he is in the yard! What if the gate is open! What if there is a hole in the fence! What if he jumps over!*

Emmy began to run. She ran into the milk house and shut the door behind her. Big Bill Byler was there. Emmy tried to stop **puffing**. She didn't want Bill to know why she had been running.

"Hi, Bill. I'm here for—for the—milk."

"I see you are," said Bill with a smile. "You sound like you are in a hurry. All right. I'll hurry and get your milk. Give me your can."

Emmy watched the cold milk gush from the big tank into her little can.

"Say, Emmy," said Bill, as he put on the lid. "Mother is making cookies. I'm going to the house in a minute. Why don't you go **along** and get some cookies to eat on the way home?"

"I guess not, thank you," said Emmy. "I ate breakfast before I came."

Emmy really did want those cookies. But if she went to the house she would need to go into the yard where King was.

Emmy took the milk can and went out

of the milk house. She saw the big black dog lying on the porch. He stood up and looked at her, but he did not bark.

Her heart began to pound-pound-pound-pound. She began to walk very fast. If only she could get out of sight before Bill went to the house. What if the dog slipped out the gate and came after her when Bill went in!

Emmy was puffing again by the time she got out on the road. She set the milk can down and rested a little.

Then she picked it up with the other hand and went on home.

The next day when Mother **handed** her the milk can, Emmy said, "Do I have to go, Mother?"

"Why, Emmy! I thought you liked to go after the milk!"

"Well, I do, but—but—I am afraid of their dog."

"Of King? King would not hurt a **mouse**," said Mother. "He likes children."

"But he is so big and runs out and barks and scares me."

"Emmy, do you think God can take care of you when you go for the milk?"

"Yes, but I'd still be afraid."

"Do you think God can help you to be **brave**?"

"I gue-e-e-s-s-s so."

"Then let's ask Him to take care of you and help you to be brave," said Mother.

Mother and Emmy held hands while Mother asked God to help Emmy to get over her fear of King.

Emmy took the milk can and started out. "Help me to be brave. Help me to be brave. Help me to be brave," she prayed as she went up Bylers' lane.

Emmy tried not to walk too fast. She did not want to be puffing when she got there this time.

No big black dog was in sight. No loud *bow-wow* set her heart pounding this time.

With a little prayer of thanks, Emmy reached the milk house. She went in and shut the door behind her.

And there sat King!

The big black dog opened his mouth in a wide smile and came up to her wagging his tail.

Emmy's eyes opened wide. Her mouth opened, too. But she clapped her hand over it and not a peep came out.

"Oh, go on, King," said Bill. "Emmy does not want you."

But King did not go on.

"He wants you to pet him. He likes children. Just pet him a little, then I will make him go out."

Emmy's heart was pounding, but she put out her hand and ran it over King's head. One time. Two times. Three times.

The long black tail wagged faster.

Emmy's heart stopped pounding.

She
petted King
again. Then
again and again.

Then she said, "You don't
need to make him go out, Bill.
I'm not afraid of him."

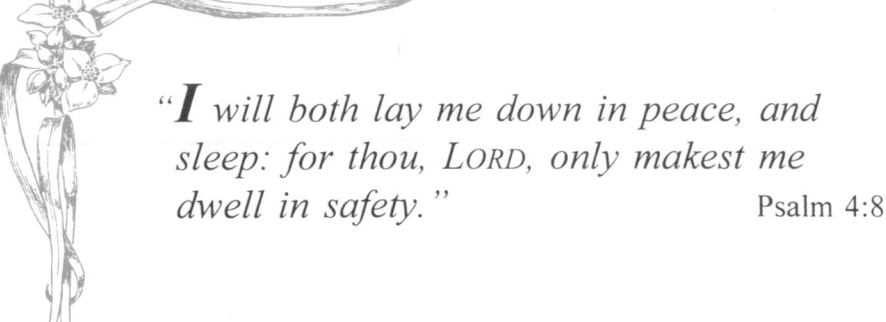

*"**I** will both lay me down in peace, and sleep: for thou, LORD, only makest me dwell in safety."*
Psalm 4:8

Story in a Story

Which story did you like best, Grandma's, or the story about Davie and Mary?

Davie and Mary were at Grandma's house. They were **staying** two days.

All day they had fun playing. Now it was night. They were in the **bunk** beds in Grandma's **spare** bedroom.

Davie **slept** on the **bottom** bunk because he was just six years old.

Mary slept on the top bunk because she was eight.

What would they do tomorrow? They had talked a long time about it. Then far away they heard, **rumble**, rumble, rumble.

"Is that thunder?" asked Davie.

"It sounded like it," answered Mary.

"I hope it doesn't come close."

"Me, too."

Rumble, rumble, rumble. This time the thunder was much closer.

Then, drop, drop, drop, came on the tin roof. Drip-drop, drip-drop-drip-drop. It was coming faster.

"It's starting to rain," whispered Davie. "I don't like thunderstorms."

RUMBLE. RUMBLE. RUMBLE.

CRASH! **Pitter**-pitter-pitter-pitter-pitter.

POUR! The rain came down with a rush.

Davie sat up. "Mary, I'm **scared**. I want to go home to Daddy and Mother."

"Hush," said Mary. "You know we can't go home now."

Thump, thump, thump, thump. Someone was coming up the stairs.

The door opened. It was Grandma.

She did not turn on the light. She came and sat on the side of the bottom bunk.

"Would you two like a story to help you go to sleep?"

"Oh, yes, Grandma," said Davie. "We are scared. Please stay here till we go to sleep."

"I'll have to see about that," said Grandma, with a laugh. "I won't promise to stay here all night, but I will tell you a story. Maybe it will put you to sleep."

"Is it a true story?" asked Davie.

"Yes, it is a true story."

"Is it a story about when you were a little girl?" asked Mary.

"Yes, it happened when I was a little girl."

"That was a long, long time ago, wasn't it?" asked Davie.

"Yes, Dear, a long, long time ago," said Grandma.

"Oh, Davie! Please stop asking questions," said Mary. "Let her tell the story!"

"Oh, all right. Go on, Grandma," said Davie.

"It was a hot summer day. I was around eight years old and my brother Tim was ten. Mother called us in from our play in the afternoon.

"She said, 'Do you think you two could go back to the woods and start the cows home? As hot as it is, a thunderstorm may come up. Then the cows will not come home by themselves. They will stay in the woods out of the storm.

"'It would be so nice if the cows were safe in the barn when Father comes home to milk.'

"Tim and I were happy to go. We felt big to go after the cows by ourselves. We had never done that before.

"'Now hurry. Don't play around,' Mama said. 'See, there are some **clouds** coming up. I am sure it is going to storm after a while. Get the cows started home as soon as you can.'

"So we went out the long field lane. It had been hot and dry that summer. The dust was deep in the lane.

"We went along through that dust kicking it high in the air with our bare feet. Then we held our breath and ran into the cloud of dust we had made.

"Grandma," cried Mary, "didn't it get on your clothes and in your hair?"

"Yes, it did," said Grandma with a laugh. "We were hot and sweaty. After running through those dust clouds, we looked awful! But the worse we looked, the more we laughed.

"Then we found a patch of **milkweeds**. The pods were just ripe.

We picked them and tore them open.
Soon the air was white with floating silk.

"A good breeze had sprung up. We
would throw the opened pods as high as
we could, then watch to see how high
and far the wind took the silk.

"Suddenly we heard a rumble,
rumble. We looked around. We saw
lightning flash down behind the woods.

"Tim cried, 'Say, Sis, did you see
that? Look, it is getting dark! We'd
better hurry!'

"We ran into the woods, 'Come Bossy,
come Bossy,' we called as loudly as we
could.

"We found the cows. They were
already standing under low trees waiting
for the storm to come.

"We got behind them. We yelled at

them. We hit them with sticks we found on the ground.

"At last we got them all started home.

"Then it began to rain. And did it ever pour! We were soaked to the skin in no time. Our hair was flat on our heads. The dust made muddy water run down our faces. We were not laughing then.

"Lightning flashed all around us. Thunder cracked. We could hardly see because it was raining so hard.

"Our clothes stuck to us. I could hardly walk in my sopping dress. The storm had cooled things off. I was shivering."

"Weren't you scared?" asked Mary.

"Indeed, I was," said Grandma. "I knew we should not be out when it was lightning. I was crying. I was scared because we had disobeyed Mama. It was getting dark and I was cold.

"Then Tim said, 'Don't cry, Sis. Let's ask God to take care of us and help us get these cows home.'

"So we stopped and prayed."

"Did God help?" asked Davie.

"Indeed, He did!" said Grandma. "We found some bigger sticks and started chasing the cows again.

Then we saw Father coming toward us. He was soaking wet, too.

"I felt so bad, I started to cry again. I knew if we had not played around we would have had the cows home before it started to rain. Father would not have had to come after us.

"Father helped us get the cows headed home. By that time it was not raining so hard anymore.

"I told Father I was sorry we had played instead of hurrying like Mama told us to.

"Tim said it was his fault because he was older than I.

"Father said we would likely remember that day for a long, long time. He said he was glad God had kept us safe. He said he was glad God had sent the rain because it was so dry."

Grandma stopped talking.

"Well, you did remember it a long time," said Davie.

"I know you were glad to get home," said Mary.

"Indeed, I was," said Grandma. "I can still remember how wonderful it felt to get into bed that night. At last I was clean and warm and dry and safe. The storm was over and the rain was falling softly."

"Hey," said Davie. "Our storm is over, too."

"Yes," said Grandma, getting up. "And the same God who took care of Tim and me is taking care of you and Mary."

"I know," said Davie. "You don't have to stay with us until we go to sleep.

We'll be all right. We'll see you in the morning. Good night, Grandma."

Why didn't the children in the story enjoy squish-squashing through the mud as the child in this poem does?

Mud

Mud is very nice to feel
All squishy-squash between the toes!
I'd rather wade in wiggly mud
Than smell a yellow rose.

Nobody else but the
    rosebush knows
How nice mud feels
    between the toes.

–Polly Chase Boyden

71

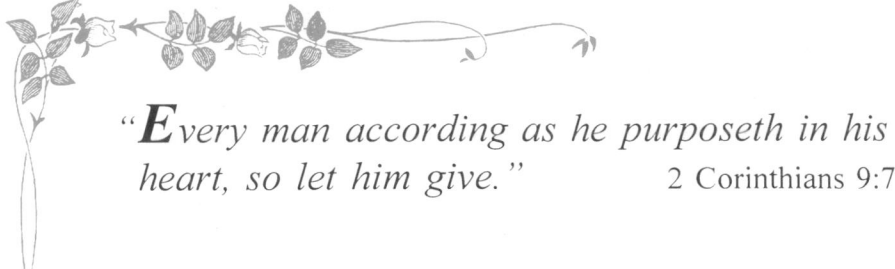

*"**E**very man according as he purposeth in his heart, so let him give."*   2 Corinthians 9:7

The Apple That Was Polished Six Times

How could the apple make so many people happy when only one person got to eat it?

John, the farmer, was picking his apples. He found one that was bigger and redder than all the rest.

"What a good-looking apple," he said. "I think I'll eat this one."

He was just ready to take a bite. Then he **thought**, *My wife would like*

*this apple. I will give
it to her.*

So he **polished** it
on his **shirt**.

The farmer's wife,
Nannie, had worked hard all
morning. By **dinnertime** she was
very **tired**.

When the farmer came in for dinner,
he said, "Nannie, you work too hard.
Here is a little **present** for you."

"Oh, how beautiful!" cried Nannie.
"Thank you, John."

After that Nannie did not feel so
tired. She sang as she worked after
dinner.

A little later she picked up the big
apple. She was just ready to take a bite.
Then she thought, *This would be a fine*

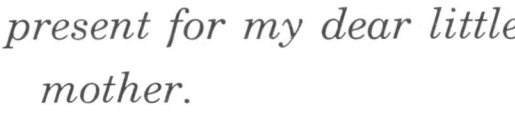

present for my dear little mother.

So she polished the apple on her apron.

Then she went to visit her dear little old mother. Her mother was sad and lonely. She was rocking on the porch.

"Hello, Mother," said Nannie.

"Hello, Nannie," said her mother.

"Mother, you sit here by yourself too much. Here is a present for you."

"Oh, how **lovely**," cried Nannie's dear little old mother. "Thank you, Nannie."

After that the little old lady sang a sweet song as she **rocked** on her porch.

Later she went into the house. "Now I will eat my apple," she said. She was just ready to take a bite. Then she thought, *This would make a fine present for the boy who brings my **groceries**. He works so hard.*

So she polished the apple on a clean white handkerchief.

When the grocery boy came up the walk with her groceries, he looked tired.

"You work too hard, Tom," said the dear little old lady. "Here is a present for you."

"What a big apple," cried Tom. "Thank you."

He put the apple into his pocket. Then he **whistled** as he went down the walk.

On his way home, he took the apple out of his pocket.

He was just ready to take a bite. Then he thought of his big sister, Sally. She was a **nurse**. *Sally would like this apple. She works so hard on the Children's Floor all day.*

This would make a fine present for her.

So he polished the apple on his **sweater**.

When Tom got home, there was Sally! Her shoes were off. She sat in a big, soft chair.

"My feet get so tired walking back and forth on the Children's Floor," she said. "The sick babies cry. The sick children fuss. And little Alice will not eat her dinner."

"You work too hard, Sally," said Tom. "Here is a present for you."

"Oh, how big and shiny!" cried Sally.

"Thank you, Tom."

Then she put on her shoes and hummed a little tune as she made supper.

Just before Sally went to bed, she thought of the apple. She went and got it. She was just ready to take a bite. Then she thought, *That little Alice-who-will-not-eat-her-dinner might eat this shiny red apple. It would be a nice present for her.*

So Sally polished the apple on the dishcloth.

The next day Nurse Sally went to work on the Children's Floor. She took the apple to Alice-who-would-not-eat-her-dinner. She said, "Here is a present for you."

"Oh, how pretty!" cried Alice-who-would-not-eat-her-dinner. "Thank you,

Nurse Sally. This apple looks good. After I eat my dinner I will eat this apple."

Then Alice-who-would-not-eat-her-dinner ate all her dinner. She polished

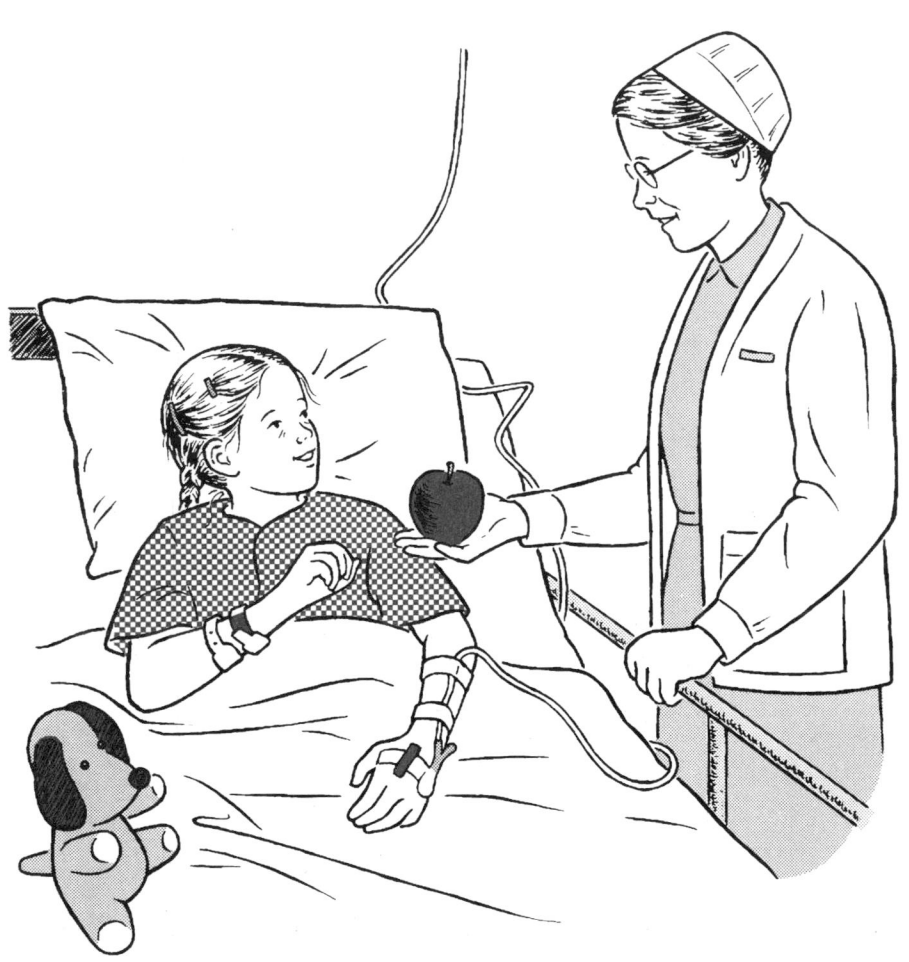

the apple on the bed sheet and ate it all too.

And she smiled for the first time in six days. She said "Thank you" again.

Later the doctor came to the Children's Floor. He looked sad and tired because he did not know what to do for Alice-who-would-not-eat-her-dinner. He was afraid she would not get well.

When he saw her he said, "Well, well, well! What has happened? I think our little Alice-who-will-not-eat-her-dinner looks much better. I think she is going to get well."

The doctor had not even seen the big red apple that had been polished six times, but he smiled and whistled as he went on down the hall.

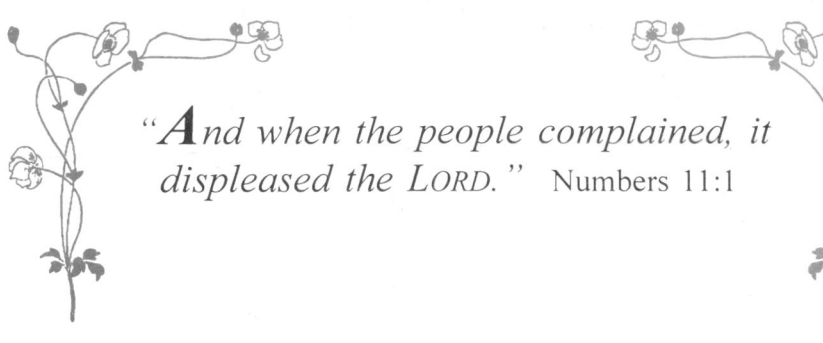

"And when the people complained, it displeased the LORD." Numbers 11:1

The Cross Box

Why didn't Ned want to use the money for the sick children?

It was raining hard. The children had to stay in the house.

"Look at all this rain," said Ned **crossly**. "I wanted to go **fishing**."

"I was going to set up my new **windmill**," **grumbled** Frank.

"The flower seeds I planted yesterday will be washed away in this hard rain,"

complained Susie. "All that work for nothing. I'll have to buy more seeds, too."

"My kitty ran away and I can't go to the barn to look for her," **sobbed** Ethel. "There is nothing in the house that is any fun to play with."

All the children felt **grouchy**. By afternoon they were very cross.

"Where are all my happy children?" said Mother. "I do not know these four little cross boxes. Now I want you to take those cross looks off your faces. Think of something **cheerful**. Not another cross word from any of you. Think of something to do that will put a smile on your faces."

For a long time the children said nothing. Then Ned smiled and went out of the room. Soon he came back with a small box. He had cut a **slot** in the top

just large enough for a dime to slip through.

"Look, Mother," he said. "Suppose we pay a dime every time we say something cross. When we get a lot of money we can buy something that will make us all happy. You will be the one to tell us if we need to put a dime in the box. We'll call it our Cross Box."

Mother laughed and said, "That is a good plan. Is everyone willing to do it?"

"I am," said Susie. "I'm not going to be cross anymore."

"**Neither** am I," said Frank. "This will be fun."

"I think so, too," said little Ethel. "I'll find something else to play with until I find my kitty."

Now Mother saw smiles on every face.

"What shall we do with all the money?" asked Susie.

"We will buy a game that all of us can play," said Ned.

"I was thinking we could buy some toys for poor children who must be in the **hospital**," said Susie.

"Oh, yes, let's," cried Ethel. "Pretty dolls for the little sick girls."

"And a big bag of candy for the boys," put in Frank.

"No, indeed. We won't do any such thing," cried Ned. "We aren't going to give this money away. We are going to buy something that will be fun for us.

"This whole thing is my idea. I am the one to say what to do with the money, or I will just **pitch** the box in the trash can!"

"Instead of doing that, you had better go and get a dime," said Mother.

Ned's mouth dropped open. His face turned red. He looked like he felt very foolish. Without another word, he brought the first dime and dropped it into the Cross Box.

How many things are getting rained on in the poem?
How many things in the picture?

Rain

The rain is raining all around,
It falls on field and tree,
It rains on the umbrellas here,
And on the ships at sea.

—Robert Louis Stevenson

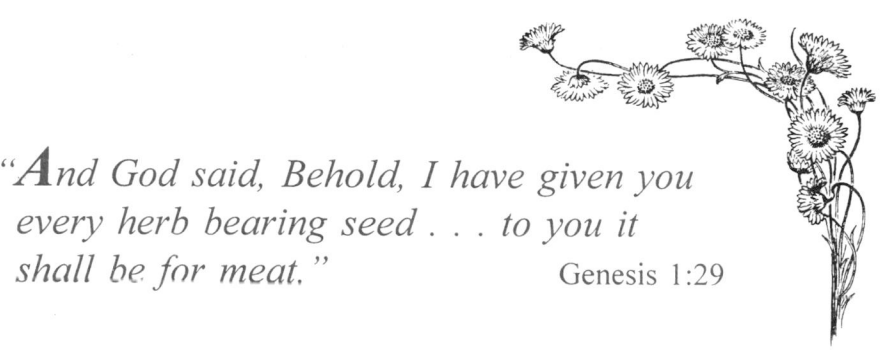

"And God said, Behold, I have given you every herb bearing seed . . . to you it shall be for meat."   Genesis 1:29

An Indian's Gift

A Story of Long Ago

How many things can you find in this story that tell you it happened long ago?

Eli was playing in front of his log house. It was spring. His father was planting **corn** in the fields.

Eli heard a noise. He looked up. An **Indian** stood close by.

"Oh, Wee-ko," cried Eli.

Wee-ko was Eli's Indian friend. The big Indian was very **friendly** to the little white boy.

It was Wee-ko who had **taught** Eli how to make and **shoot** a **bow** and **arrow**. It was Wee-ko who had taught him how to fish.

Eli's father was too busy to go fishing. He had to work in the fields from morning until night. There would be no food if he did not work.

This morning Wee-ko gave Eli a **handful** of seeds. He made a little hole in the ground and planted one of the seeds. He showed Eli how to plant the rest of the seeds in the same way. Then he went away into the **forest**.

Eli **wondered** what the seeds could be. They looked a little like corn, but he had never seen such small round grains of corn. What could they be?

That night Eli showed the seeds to his father. His father said, "It looks a little like corn, but it can't be corn. The seeds are too small.

"There is just one way to find out what they are, son. Plant them and let them **grow**. But don't feel too bad if they do not grow."

The next day Eli planted the rest of the seeds in his own little garden.

After a while the seeds came up. The little green shoots grew higher and higher. They looked like the corn growing in his father's fields. But his father's corn had grown higher than Eli's head. His own plants did not reach to his shoulder.

The rain and the sun made the plants

grow. But always his father's corn grew faster.

At last, tiny ears grew on Eli's plants. He was sure now that it was corn, but why were the ears so small? Why was his corn so short? His father's corn was much taller.

"It surely is corn," said his father. "But Wee-ko must have given you poor seeds. That is the reason the plants are so small."

Eli felt very sad. He wondered why his Indian friend had given him such poor seeds. He did not want to hurt Wee-ko's feelings, but the corn was too small to **bother** with.

At the end of summer Eli's father cut his corn. Eli left his standing in the garden. "Let the birds have it if they want it," Eli said.

When the snow began to fly, Wee-ko came again. He saw the corn standing in the garden. He broke off one of the little dried ears. He pulled the dried up husks off the ear. Then he rubbed some of the seed off the ear into his hand.

Wee-ko laid some dry leaves and sticks on a flat rock. He asked Eli to get him fire. Eli went into the cabin. Soon he came back carrying a lighted stick.

Wee-ko lit the leaves and sticks on the rock. As the fire burned he put on more wood.

When the rock was hot, Wee-ko put out the fire and pushed off the wood. Then he dropped the grains of corn on the hot rock. Eli watched him. What was Wee-ko doing?

With a long stick he stirred the corn.

Then, Pop! Pop! Pop! went the corn.

Eli's eyes got big. At every pop a corn grain hopped up and turned big and fluffy white. Soon the rock was covered with white, fluffy, popped corn.

Wee-ko took some of it in his hands and ate it. He gave some to Eli. Then he went away into the forest.

Eli tasted the popped corn. Then he understood. His friend had given him a new kind of corn—corn which went "pop" when it got hot.

Eli got a basket and knife and headed for the garden.

It didn't take him long to cut all the corn in his garden. His mother popped some in a pan over the fire in the fireplace.

Eli's family ate popped corn many times that winter. But they did not eat it all. Eli carefully packed some of the seeds into a small leather bag. When spring came, he would plant popcorn in his garden again.

The story told us about the different things Eli did in the spring, summer, fall, and winter. This poem gives a different color to each season. Are they the colors you would give to the seasons where you live?

Four Seasons

Springtime is a green time
    When seedlings start their growing.
Summertime's a rainbow time
    When many blooms are blowing.
Autumntime's a brown time
    When seeds are ripe for sowing;
But wintertime's a white time
    (It is the flowers' nighttime)
When stars of frost are glowing.

–Rowena Bennett

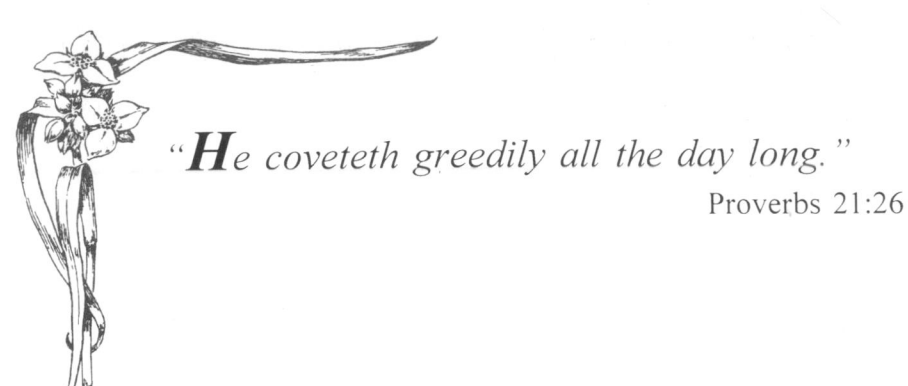

Good-bye, Little Blue Jeep

At the end of this story, do you think David still wanted to be friends with Tim?

Sometimes you want something the minute you see it. Then you just forget all about what is right to do. You think only of a way to get what you want.

That is how it was when David came over to Tim's house. David had a box of little toy **vehicles**.

The minute David **dumped** them on the floor, Tim thought, *I wish they were mine! Oh, I wish they were mine!*

There were all kinds of vehicles: dump trucks, milk trucks, **jeeps**, big cars, little cars, fire trucks, and flat-bed trucks.

"My mother got them at a yard sale," said David. "They are not new, but not one of them is **broken**. There must be twenty or **thirty** here. I **haven't** even counted them."

From then on, every minute that he and David were playing, Tim was thinking, *I wish they were mine. Oh, I wish they were mine.*

Tim really did not plan to keep any of the little vehicles. It just seemed to happen that way.

When it was time for David to go home, they put all the trucks and cars back into the box. After David had left, Tim saw one they had missed. A little blue jeep lay behind the table leg.

Tim pulled it out and stood holding it in his hand.

He has so many, he thought. *He will not know that one is missing. He will not remember there was a blue jeep.*

Tim began playing with the little jeep. But in a minute, **through** the window, he saw David coming back. He put the jeep into his pocket and went to the door.

"Tim," cried David. "I have lost one of my vehicles. That little blue jeep. Do you remember seeing it?"

"Yes, I remember it," said Tim. "Did

you lose it? That is too bad. Maybe you lost it on the way home."

"No, I held the box under my **arm** all the way. Do you remember putting it into the box? Do you remember picking it up?"

"No, I don't," said Tim.

"Then it must be here yet. Please help me look for it."

David looked here. He looked there. He looked everywhere.

Tim looked too. He looked here. He looked there. He looked everywhere. But all the time he had his hand on the little blue jeep in his pocket.

At last David gave up and went home.

By that time Tim was feeling pretty bad. But he thought, *I can't help it if his jeep got lost at my house. David should have found it and taken it home. It is just too bad that he did not see it.*

The little blue jeep did not make Tim as happy as he thought it would. It did not make him happy at all.

He had to play with it in his room because he was afraid his mother would see it. He had to remember to keep it **hidden**.

The next day when Tim saw David, he thought he would say, "I found your jeep. I looked for it again after you went home." But he could not say it. That would not be the **truth**. David might guess that he had had the blue jeep all the time.

What made me keep it? Tim thought over and over. *What ever made me keep it?*

As the days went by, Tim felt bad. He did not want to play with the little jeep anymore. He did not want to play with David anymore. He did not even want to be near him. He was afraid David would say something about the jeep.

One day he thought, *I have lost my best friend all because of that blue jeep. I have not been happy one minute since*

I kept it. David and I will never be friends again unless I take it back and tell him what I did.

Tim knew he should take the jeep back; but how could he ever do it?

Taking the jeep from David had been so **easy**. Taking it back would be the **hardest** thing he had ever done.

Then he thought of a way. After school his mother said he could go to David's house. When David came to the door, Tim asked, "Can we play with your little vehicles today?"

"That is what I am doing right now," said David. "Come on in."

When Tim sat down to play, David went out for something.

Tim thought, *When David comes back, I will hand him the jeep and tell him*

what I did. I will tell him I am sorry.
I know we cannot be friends until I do
that.

Tim took the jeep
out of his pocket
and looked at it.

"Good-bye, little
blue jeep. The next
time I want something that is not mine,
I will remember you."

*When you play with toy cars, can you make all
the different sounds this poem tells about?*

Funny the Way
Different Cars Start

Funny the way
Different cars start.
Some with a chunk and a jerk,
Some with a cough and a puff
of smoke
Out of the back,
Some with only a little click—
with hardly any noise.

Funny the way

Different cars run.

Some rattle and bang,

Some whirrr,

Some knock and knock.

Some purr

And hummmmm

Smoothly on

    with hardly any noise.

–Dorothy Baruch

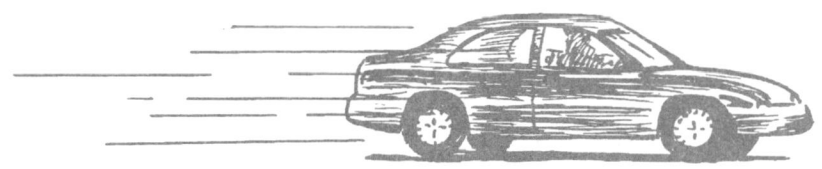

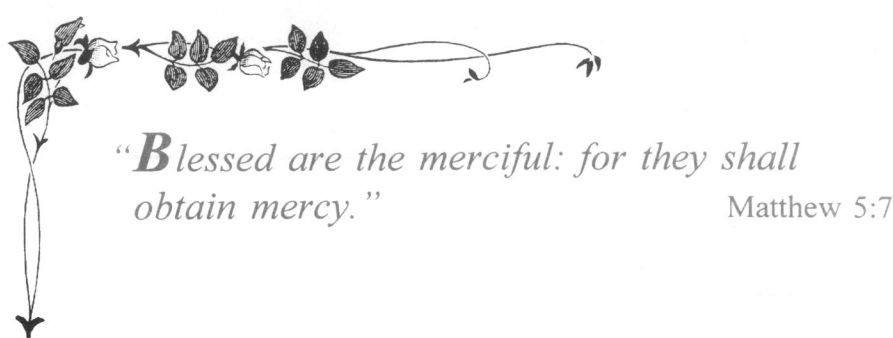

*"**B**lessed are the merciful: for they shall obtain mercy."* Matthew 5:7

Why Henry Was Late

A Story of Long Ago

Can you guess how people got milk in the city at the time of this story?

Henry was on his way to school one morning. He was hurrying. He had not been late to school one time yet, and he did not want to break his good **record**.

Then he saw a little boy standing on the sidewalk. He was **crying**, so Henry stopped.

"What is the matter, little **fellow**?" he asked.

"I can't find my way home," sobbed the boy.

"What is your name? Where do you live?" Henry asked next.

"My name is Burt Strong. I live on Gray Street."

"Gray Street! That is a long way from here."

"I know. I can't remember how to get there."

"Why are you so far from home, Burt?"

"Mother said I could ride with the **milkman** for a little way. I rode too far. Now I don't know the turns going back."

"Well, I wish I had time to take you home, but I must go on to school. I will be late if I don't hurry. You just go down this street for three blocks. Then turn left and go two blocks. Then ask someone how to go the rest of the way. It wouldn't be too far."

The little fellow began to cry again. "Oh, please take me home. I can't remember where to turn. I'm scared I'll get lost again."

Henry stood still for a few **moments**. "Oh, dear," he said to himself. "I haven't been late this **whole** year. It is not my **fault** this boy is lost. He should have known better than to ride this far. But I can't go off and leave him."

At last he said, "I'll take you home if you stop crying. I don't want to walk with a boy who is crying. Don't you know big boys shouldn't cry?"

Burt stopped crying. "If I **hadn't** been crying you would have gone on to school and I never would have gotten home."

"You are right about that," said Henry with a laugh. "**Perhaps** boys your **size** can cry sometimes. Let's hurry. I do not want to be any later than I must."

It was a long walk back to Burt's street. As soon as the little fellow saw his house in the distance, he thanked Henry and began to run.

Henry turned and ran too. He was **fifteen** minutes late. He felt really bad when he walked into the schoolroom.

When he told his teacher the **reason**, she smiled. "You did right, Henry. The Bible teaches us to be kind. It does not say you should never for any reason be late for school," she said.

Henry smiled too. He didn't feel bad anymore.

"He that hath mercy on the poor, happy is he."

Proverbs 14:21

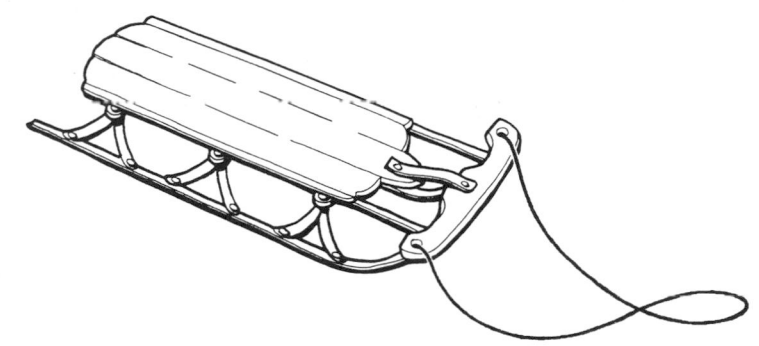

Helping Hands

What do you think happened that made Harold stop and go back to the old woman?

Harold **hurried** home from school one **snowy** day. His **playmates** had taken their sleds to coast on Pine Hill.

He wanted to go too, unless his mother needed him to do something for her when he got home.

Harold's mother said he could go.

He **grabbed** his sled and ran down the walk.

As Harold hurried along the street he saw an old woman **ahead** of him. She carried a big **basket** of clothes. She walked very **carefully** on the icy sidewalk.

Harold ran past her. But in a few minutes he stopped. Slowly he turned and went back to the old woman.

She had put down her basket and was **resting** upon a **doorstep**. He stopped and said, "Good afternoon, Ma'am."

"I suppose it is a good afternoon for boys who like to slide," she said. "But I do not like to slide on ice. I am afraid I shall fall with my basket before I get home."

"Put your basket on my sled. I will take it home for you," said Harold.

"What!" said the old woman. "Are you making fun of me?"

"No, Ma'am," said Harold. "I never make fun of old **people**. I will be glad to take it home for you."

A happy look came onto the face of the old woman. She got up. Harold put the basket on his sled. Then off they started.

Harold went very slowly because the old woman could not walk very fast.

Soon they met one of Harold's friends on his way to Pine Hill.

"Hello, Harold, I thought you were going **coasting** with us."

"I am," laughed Harold, "but I am running a **delivery** wagon right now."

"So I see," said the boy. "Well, I am off to the hill." Away he went.

"I will be there soon," Harold called after him.

He came to the place where the old woman lived. He carried the basket of clothes into the house for her.

"God bless you, young man," said the woman with tears in her eyes. "Not many boys would give up the fun of coasting to help an old woman. Thank you, thank you."

"You are welcome," said Harold. He took his sled and ran off to the hill.

For some reason Harold thought coasting was extra fun the rest of that afternoon.

The hill in this poem could well be Pine Hill in the story. It tells what you see when a snowy hill and children with sleds get together.

Coasting

Frosty is the morning; but the sun
is bright,
Flooding all the landscape with its
golden light.
Hark the sounds of laughter and of
voices shrill!
See the happy children coasting down
the hill.

There are Tom and Charley, and their
sister Nell;
There are John and Willie, Kate and
Isabel.
Eyes with pleasure beaming, cheeks
with health aglow;
Bless the merry children playing in
the snow.

Now I hear them shouting, "Ready!
  Clear the track!"

Down the slope they're rushing, now
  they're trotting back.

Full of fun and frolic, thus they come
  and go;

Coasting down the hillside, trudging
  through the snow.

—Author Unknown

*"**D**epart from evil, and do good."*

Psalm 34:14

It Is Up to You

What did Billy learn by the end of the story?

On Saturday morning all the children on the street were playing in Betty King's yard. They played on the swings. They played on the **slide** and merry-go-round.

That is, all but Billy. He sat all by **himself** on the **steps** of his own back porch. He did not look happy. In **fact**, he looked cross.

Mother came out. "Why, Billy," she said. "I thought you were over at Betty's playing with the other children."

"I was," said Billy **glumly**.

"Well, what happened? Why **aren't** you over there now?"

"Mrs. King sent me home. I'm **never** going to play there again."

Mother sat down on the steps beside Billy. "Tell me what happened. Why did Mrs. King send you home?"

"She just **doesn't** like me," said Billy.

"Now, Billy, you know better than that," said Mother. "Tell me what you did."

"Well, all I did was take the swing away from those little girls. They are such **slowpokes**. When it is their turn to have the swing, they just fool around."

Mother looked sad. She said, "When it is their turn, they should be able to play with the swing any way they please. You play with it the way you want to when it's your turn, don't you?"

Billy said nothing.

"Is that all you did?"

"I pushed Jimmy a little. He fell down and **skinned** his knee. It didn't **bleed** much, but he cried like a baby."

"Why did you push him?" asked Mother.

"He was in my way. I wanted to go up the slide ladder and he just stood there. He didn't know if he wanted to go up or not. Anyway, he didn't have to make such a fuss over nothing."

"I understand why Mrs. King sent you home," said Mother. "Betty likes to have the children over in her yard. Her mother lets them come because she knows they **enjoy** playing there. But if one child makes the others unhappy, why should she let him play there? He spoils the fun for everyone."

Billy said nothing.

"Did Betty's mother say you could never come back?"

"No. She said I could come when I could play nicely."

"Well then, Billy, it is up to you, isn't it? You can play nicely if you want to. It's up to you. You go back over and play when you are ready to play nicely. And I think Daddy and I will want to talk to you some more this evening."

Mother got up and went back into the house.

Billy sat for a long time. Then he got up and went around the house. He sat on the front porch steps. From there he could see the children playing in Kings' yard. From their shouts and laughter, he could tell they were having a lot of fun.

He wished he were over there having fun, too. He wished he hadn't acted so mean. But he couldn't go back after Mrs. King had sent him home.

Then he remembered what Mother had said. She had said it was up to him.

"I guess maybe it is," Billy said to himself.

He got up and went across the street. Would the children let him play?

He stood at the edge of the yard and watched the others. Then he saw Janie,

the smallest girl. She was sitting at the top of the slide. She wanted to go down but she was afraid.

Billy ran to the bottom of the slide. He held out his arms. He called, "Let go, Janie. I'll catch you."

"Don't you do it, Janie," cried Sally. "He will let you fall. He will hurt you like he did Jimmy a while ago!"

"No, I won't," said Billy. "I really will catch you."

But Janie held on till Sally went and helped her down.

Billy turned to the swings. One of the girls was just sitting there. Her legs were too short to reach the ground.

"Here, I'll push you, Pam," said Billy. "I'm sorry I took the swing away from you. I'm going to play nicely now."

"You let me alone!" cried Pam. "I don't want you to push me."

Billy walked away feeling cross. The children had not forgotten how mean he had been. Now they would not let him show that he wanted to be nice.

Then he thought, *I guess I was the one who made them afraid of me. I did only a few mean things, but now they don't trust me. It is going to take a long time before they like me again. It is all up to me.*

It didn't seem fair, but that's the way it was.

Just then he saw Jimmy. The little boy was climbing up the slide ladder on the underside. He was halfway up when his foot slipped. All at once he was hanging in the air by only one hand.

"Someone help me!" he cried.

Betty screamed.

Billy dashed to the slide. He reached up and put his arms around Jimmy's legs.

"I've got you, Jimmy," he said. "Let go and slide down against me. I won't let you fall."

"Yes, you will," cried Jimmy. "Somebody else come, quick!"

But Billy hung on and then Jimmy's other hand let loose. He slid down against Billy's body. Billy held him tightly so that he didn't land hard at all.

He smiled up at Billy. "Thanks, Billy. I was really scared."

"That's all right," said Billy. "Come on. Let's go down the slide. You go first."

As he went up the ladder behind

Jimmy, Billy saw Mrs. King standing there. She must have run out when Betty screamed.

"Billy kept him from getting hurt," Betty was saying.

Mrs. King smiled up at him and he smiled down at her.

"Maybe it won't take as long as I thought," Billy said to himself, as he watched Jimmy go down the slide.

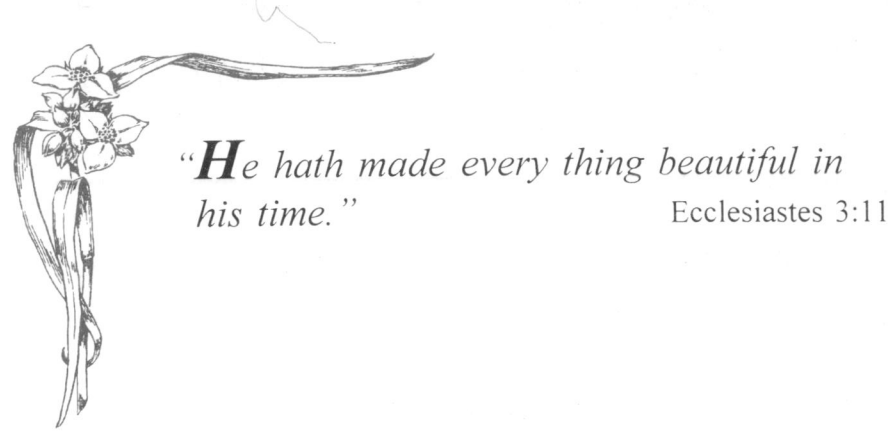

Baby Insect

In two stages of the insect's life it does not move. As you read this story, try to find out what those two stages are.

On his way to school one morning, Kurt found a **caterpillar**. It was on a milkweed plant. It had yellow and white and black **stripes**.

"Here is a caterpillar," he said to himself.

"I will take it to school. Maybe Miss Lee can tell what kind it is. Maybe she will let me keep it in school. We can **watch** it grow."

"Yes, you may keep it," said Miss Lee. "Here is a jar. It has a lid so the caterpillar cannot get out. There are **holes** in the lid so it can get air. You must feed it once a day."

"I will get it some grass," said Bill.

"I will get it some tree leaves," said Sue.

"No, it will not eat those," said Miss Lee. "You must feed it leaves from the **plant** you found it on."

"I never knew you had to do that," said Bill. "I thought caterpillars ate anything green."

Every day Kurt brought fresh leaves

from the milkweed plant. Every day the children watched the striped caterpillar eat the milkweed leaves.

"Isn't it beautiful with those black and yellow and white stripes!"

"Where did the caterpillar come from? How big will it grow? It is lots bigger now than when we first got it."

"What will it do after it gets big?"

"Will we need a bigger jar?"

"Wait a minute," cried Miss Lee. She held up her hands. "You have too many **questions**. This caterpillar came from a tiny egg.

"It is a baby **insect**. You must wait and see how big it grows and what it will do."

"An insect! Didn't you tell us an insect has six legs? This caterpillar has more than six legs."

Miss Lee laughed. "It is just a baby now. Wait and see how it turns out. No, it will not need a bigger jar."

"What kind of insect laid the egg?" asked Sue.

"Will some of its legs fall off until it has just six?"

"How soon will it grow into a big insect?"

"Just wait and see," laughed Miss Lee. "That is the best way to find out. Only God could make an insect that grows like this one."

One morning Kurt brought fresh leaves. He opened the jar. The caterpillar was not there.

"Miss Lee, the caterpillar is gone," he cried.

Miss Lee and all the children hurried to look in the jar.

"It got out," said Sue.

"Did you put the lid on right when you fed it the last time?" asked Bob.

"Yes," said Kurt, "The lid was tight."

"Look on the inside of the lid," said Miss Lee.

A little green case with tiny gold dots hung on the lid.

"Oh, oh, a cocoon!" cried

the children. "The caterpillar made a cocoon. Isn't it beautiful!"

"No, children, this is not a cocoon.

It is a **chrysalis**. Moths come out of cocoons, but a butterfly will come out of a chrysalis."

"Miss Lee, the caterpillar was striped. The chrysalis is green. Will the insect be striped or green?"

"Wait and see," said Miss Lee.

"Now it does not have any legs at all," said Bill. "Is it still an insect?"

"Yes, it is still an insect, but it is not grown yet. It goes through four **stages** before it is grown. First it was a tiny egg. Then the egg hatched into a caterpillar. The caterpillar turned into this chrysalis. The next stage will be the last one. Then it will be a grown-up insect.

"If we watch it, maybe we will see it go from this third stage to the fourth one."

Now Kurt did not have to bring milkweed leaves. The chrysalis just hung there. The children looked at it every day.

One morning Kurt said, "Miss Lee, something is wrong with the chrysalis. It is not pretty and green like it was. It is brown. Do you think it died?"

The children ran to look. Miss Lee came too. "No, it has not died," she said. "It is getting ready to come out. I'm glad we can watch it."

Soon the chrysalis split down the side. Something brown and **wrinkled** and wet came out.

"What kind of insect is that?" asked Kurt.

"It looks a little like a **butterfly**; but its wings are not right. They are all wrinkled," said Sue.

"Yes, it is a butterfly. We must wait. Its wings will be all right when they dry."

The butterfly just sat there. Then it began to move its wings up and down, up and down, up and down. Soon they were big and dry. They were not wrinkled anymore. They were a beautiful rusty orange and black.

"I can see six legs now," said Sue. "How did all those caterpillar legs turn out to be only six butterfly legs?"

"Only God knows that," said Kurt.

"It is a full-grown insect now," said Miss Lee. "It will soon lay eggs on a milkweed plant, just like its mother did. That is stage one. Who can tell me what will happen then?"

"A caterpillar will come out of every egg. That is stage two," said Bill.

"Each of those caterpillars will eat and eat until it is big. Then it will turn into a chrysalis," said Bob. "That is stage three."

"A butterfly like this one will hatch out of the chrysalis. It will lay more eggs on another milkweed," said Sue.

"Good," said Miss Lee. "I see you know the four stages. That is just what will happen."

"What I want to know," said one of the children, "is how that striped caterpillar could turn itself into this orange and black butterfly. Once it was a tiny egg. Now look at it. How did it do it?"

"No one in the world knows that. All we know is that God made it that way," said Miss Lee.

"This is a **monarch** butterfly. The caterpillar could not turn into another kind of butterfly even if it wanted to. All the eggs it lays will turn into monarch butterflies like this one."

"Why don't butterflies have baby butterflies like cats and dogs have babies?" asked Bill.

"Why don't they sit on their eggs and hatch them like hens do?" asked Bob.

The children all laughed.

Miss Lee said, "We cannot know why God made things like He did. Maybe those are questions we should not ask. We do know that everything He made is wonderful. There is not one single thing that man knows everything about.

"Many insects help us in different ways, but I think God made lots of them just for pretty—just for us to enjoy, like this butterfly."

"Open the door! Open the door!" cried Kurt. "It is going to fly!"

The butterfly took off from the jar lid. Out through the open door into the sunshine it fluttered.

"Good-bye, good-bye," called the children. They kept looking until the butterfly flew up over the trees and out of sight.

*These four poems tell about some of the things
God made. Some of those things are alive and some
are not. Can you point them out?*

All Things Bright
and Beautiful

All things bright and beautiful,
All creatures great and small,
All things wise and wonderful—
The Lord God made them all.

Each little flower that opens,
Each little bird that sings—
He made their glowing colors,
He made their tiny wings.

The purple-headed mountain,
The river running by,
The morning and the sunset
That lighteth up the sky,

140

The tall trees in the greenwood,
The pleasant summer sun,
The ripe fruits in the garden—
He made them every one.

He gave us eyes to see them,
And lips that we might tell
How great is God Almighty,
Who hath made all things well.

—C. F. Alexander

The Cricket

And when the rain had gone away
And it was shining everywhere,
I ran out on the walk to play
And found a little bug was there.

And he was running just as fast
As any little bug could run,
Until he stopped for breath at last,
All black and shiny in the sun.

And then he chirped a song to me
And gave his wings a little tug,
And *that's* the way he showed
   that he
Was very glad to be a bug!

—Marjorie Barrows

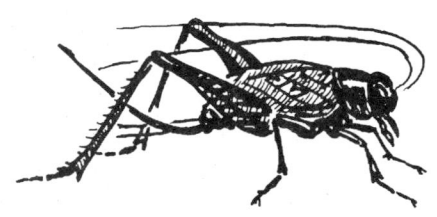

A Cricket

In a matchbox
is a cricket
    with a patent-leather shine.
It's at Peter's,
and he's printed
MISTER CRICKET on a sign.

In a fruit jar
that is open,
with a leaf on which to dine,
is a cricket
that is Kathy's
    and she thinks it's very fine.

Nothing's gayer
than a cricket!
Nothing's louder after nine!
But my mother
thinks a *thicket*
is the nicest place for mine.

                        –Aileen Fisher

Fuzzy Wuzzy,
Creepy Crawly

Fuzzy wuzzy, creepy crawly
   Caterpillar funny,
You will be a butterfly
   When the days are sunny.

Winging, flinging, dancing, springing
   Butterfly so yellow,
You were once a caterpillar,
   Wiggly, wiggly fellow.

—Lillian Schultz

Captain or Deck Hand?

Can you find out why Lester
did not want to play on the ship anymore?

"Boys, I need your help this morning," said Daddy.

"Good!" cried Roy. He was seven. He liked to work with Daddy.

"What are you going to do?" asked Lester. He was five. He liked to work with Daddy, too.

145

"I am going to pull down the old **rail** fence behind the barn. You boys can help carry rails."

Daddy drove the tractor. Roy and Lester rode in the wagon behind the tractor.

It was not hard to pull down the fence. It was old and falling down. They **stacked** the rails on the wagon.

Then they rode on top of the **pile** to a place behind the shed.

"We will stack them against the back of the shed," said Daddy. "But first I will **drive** in two **stakes** out from the shed a little way. Then we can pile the rails high and they won't roll down. That way we can mow close to the stack."

Roy and Lester had fun carrying the rails to Daddy. They stacked them higher and higher between the shed and the stakes.

"There," said Daddy, as he put on the last rail, "that job is done. Thanks for your help, boys."

"What a high stack!" said Lester. "May we climb on it?"

"Yes, this would be a good place to play," said Daddy.

Roy looked at the pile. He said, "It looks like a ship, doesn't it? We can **pretend** it is a ship."

"That is a good idea," said Daddy. "You could pretend it is a ship or a mountain, or a lighthouse or a trailer truck, or lots of other things."

"We will play that it is a ship first," said Roy to Lester. "And I will be the **captain**."

"What does the captain do?" asked Lester.

"He is the boss of the ship. He **steers** it. He tells the **deck** hand what to do."

"What is a deck hand?" asked Lester.

"He is the one who does the work on the deck. He does anything the captain tells him to do. You will be the deck hand."

"No, I want to be a captain, too," said Lester.

"Oh, no! A ship has only one captain," said Roy. "I'm the captain because I said so first. Anyhow, it was my idea."

"Now, Roy," said Daddy. "You must take turns if both of you want to be captain."

"All right, we'll take turns," said Roy.

Daddy climbed onto the tractor. "You two have fun. If you get seasick, lie down on the deck. Don't fall overboard."

Roy and Lester laughed. They waved good-bye to Daddy as he drove away.

"Now let's fix up our ship," said Roy. "We need a **wheel** to steer with. We need a **flag** and a box for our food. And we need some fishing lines."

The boys looked in the shed and walked around hunting for things they could use.

Lester found a rope. "We can use this for a fishing line," he said.

"This old hubcap would make a good wheel," said Roy. "And look at this!" he cried, picking up a tin can. "This will be my **telescope**."

He put it to his eye. "Yes, this will be a fine telescope. "You find the rest of the stuff, Lester. I must get on the ship. I must see if any other ships are coming."

Roy climbed on the stack of rails. He put the tin can to one eye.

"Oh, I see another ship. It is coming this way!"

"Let me see. I want to look through the telescope, too."

"No, no. Only the captain looks through the telescope. You are the deck hand. Bring up the ship's wheel and the fishing line."

Lester brought the things to the top of the pile.

"I want to see the other ship. Please let me," he begged.

Roy laughed. "I am only pretending. I don't see a real ship. Anyway, only the captain uses the telescope."

"Let me be captain, then," begged Lester. "Daddy said we must take turns being captain."

"Well, today is my turn," said Roy.

"All day?" asked Lester in a sad voice.

"Yes. You can be captain all day tomorrow."

"What can I do now?"

"You can run to the house and ask Mother for something to use for a flag. A ship needs a flag," said Roy.

Lester climbed down and ran to the house.

Roy laid the telescope down. He fixed the hubcap at the front of the ship against one of the rails.

Soon Lester came climbing to the top of the pile.

"See where I put the ship's wheel," said Roy. "You can't really turn it, of course. Don't touch it or it will fall down. Anyway, steering is the captain's job."

Lester held out an old shirt. "Mother tied it to the stick for us," he said.

"Hey, that's a neat flag," cried Roy. He grabbed it out of Lester's hand. "It's the captain's job to wave the flag."

Roy went to the highest place on the pile. He looked through the telescope. He held his arm high and waved the flag. He shouted at the top of his voice. "Hey, there! Ho, there, you other ship. Where are you going? We are going to Africa!"

Lester watched Roy for a minute.

Then he climbed down from the stack of rails. "I don't want to play anymore," he said.

"Why not?" asked Roy, in surprise.

"Because there isn't anything to do. It's no fun for me when the captain does everything. It's no fun for me when you are so selfish." He walked away.

"Go on then! I don't care! I'll play alone!" Roy shouted, as Lester went out of sight around the shed.

Roy went on playing captain. He steered the ship through the waves. He waved the flag back and forth. He looked through the telescope. He saw some more ships. He shouted to other captains.

And there wasn't anything else to do.

I can't sit here and wave this old shirt

154

all the time, Roy thought. *I can't keep looking through this old tin can.*

He laid down the flag and telescope. He sat still for a long time. Then he said, right out loud, "It is no fun for me, either, when the captain does everything. Even when I am the captain."

I wonder where Lester is, he thought. *I'll go see what he is doing.*

Roy found his little brother playing in the sandbox.

Lester looked up, but he did not smile. Then he went on playing.

Roy stood watching him for a while. Then he said, "I'm sorry I was so selfish, Lester. You can be captain now, if you want to. It's no fun playing on the ship by myself. Will you play with me?"

"Oh, yes!" cried Lester. He jumped up,

throwing sand every which way. "Let's go! It's no fun playing in the sandbox all by myself, either."

Soon Captain Lester was chasing another ship, and Roy the deck hand was pulling a big whale up on the deck.

"For he knoweth the secrets of the heart."

Psalm 44:21

Lesson of the Lincoln Logs

Part 1

Some secrets are fun to keep.
Did Bradley have a good secret?

Mother hung up the telephone. "That was Aunt Ella," she said, as she came back to the supper table. "Her mother **died**. She must go to Ohio and will be away for a week. She must help take care of her mother's things. She asked if we will take care of Timmy **until** she comes back."

"Isn't Uncle Tim going?" asked Daddy.

"Yes, he will take her, but he must come right back. He can't stay away from his work that long."

"Why can't she take Timmy along?" asked Bradley. He liked his little **cousin**, but he **wasn't** sure about having him around for a week.

"She said she can't look after a three-year-old and get all the work done. There is no place she can leave him in Ohio.

"He will stay here only in the daytime. Uncle Tim will pick him up after work and keep him at night. Then he will drop him off on his way to work in the morning."

"Of course he can stay here," said Daddy. "Timmy has been here many times. He will make out just fine. With Bradley to play with, he won't miss his mother so much."

"I'll be in school most of the day," said Bradley.

"I know, but your toy closet is full of toys. He will be happy playing by himself till you get home," said Mother.

"But I don't want him in my room when I'm in school," cried Bradley. "Every time he comes he gets into everything! He might **spoil** or lose something."

"Like what?" asked Mother.

"Like my birthday present. I don't want him playing with my Lincoln Logs. Anyway, Timmy doesn't know I have them. He doesn't need to play with them. I haven't played with them much, myself."

"I was thinking he would have the most fun with them," said Mother. "He could build things and **load** them on the trucks. He couldn't hurt them. They are made of wood."

"He might break the roof pieces or lose something."

"Now, Bradley," Daddy said, "those roof pieces are made of **plastic**. Timmy couldn't break them. You are acting selfish. If you have something that he could break, just put it up on your closet **shelf**."

"Couldn't Timmy play out in the yard with Rocket until I get home from school? Then I could take care of my things."

"No, that puppy is too big and **rough**," said Mother. "The last time

Timmy was here Rocket jumped up on him and knocked him down. He **chewed** on Timmy's shoe. Then he grabbed his cap and ran off and chewed on that. Rocket is too rough for Timmy. He will not want to play in the yard if the puppy is around."

"Can't you pen Rocket up? Then Timmy can play in the sandbox and on the swing and slide."

"Yes, Rocket can be penned up so Timmy can play in the yard," said Daddy. "But he will want to play with your toys, too. He can't hurt those Lincoln Logs. You will not have any fun at all this week if you act so selfish with your things. Remember, Bradley, selfish people are never happy."

That night before Bradley went to bed he opened the door to his toy closet.

His trucks and cars and tractors sat in a nice row. And there were his building blocks, his farm set and his new birthday present—the box of Lincoln Logs. They were in a nice row, too. Bradley knew what the closet would look like after Timmy played in it.

"Timmy can play with all my other toys. But I don't want him playing with my Lincoln Logs," he said to himself as he got into bed.

* * * * *

"When is Timmy coming?" asked Bradley at the breakfast table the next morning.

"He will be here when you get home from school," said Mother.

After breakfast Bradley went up to his room to get ready for school. He opened the door of his toy closet. He picked up

163

the box of Lincoln Logs. Where could he hide it?

He looked at the top shelf. No, Timmy would see it there.

He looked all around his room. There was no safe place there.

Bradley went down the back stairs. He went out the back door into the yard.

Rocket came running and jumped up on him. He almost knocked the box of Lincoln Logs out of his arms. Bradley pushed him away and went into the tool-shed. He shut the door in Rocket's face.

Now, where could he put the box? He looked all around. At last he found a good place. It was back in the corner, under the shelf, behind the blue plastic **sheet** Daddy put on the woodpile in the winter. Timmy would not see the box there, even if he went into the shed.

*"**G**od is a . . . revealer of secrets."* Daniel 2:47

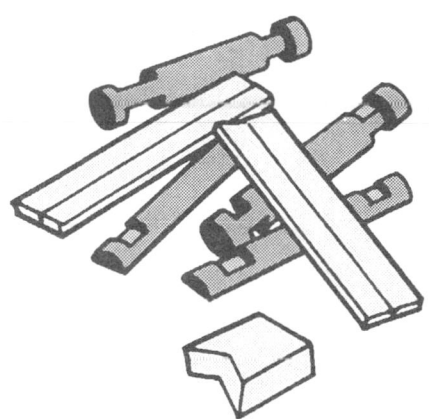

Lesson of the Lincoln Logs

Part 2

What lesson did Bradley learn?

Every day that week, Timmy was waiting for Bradley when he got home from school. Then Bradley played with him.

Sometimes he helped Timmy play with the toys in the toy closet. Downstairs Mother would hear Timmy laughing and talking. But she never heard Bradley.

Sometimes Bradley would pen up Rocket and play with Timmy in the sandbox or on the swing or slide. Through the window Mother would hear Timmy laughing and shouting. But she never heard Bradley.

When Timmy went back into the house, Bradley would let Rocket out of the shed. The big puppy would tear out and jump up on him. He would chew on his shoe.

Bradley would not pet Rocket or even talk to him. He would push him away and go into the house and play with Timmy until Uncle Tim came for him. Then he would go upstairs and put his toys in nice rows again.

Friday came at last. Aunt Ella would be home tomorrow. Bradley came home from school. One more time he penned up Rocket and played with Timmy in the sandbox.

That evening when Uncle Tim came for his little son, Timmy didn't want to go with him.

"Can't I stay and live with Bradley?" he asked.

Uncle Tim laughed. "I see it is time to get this little boy home to his mother or he will forget who he belongs to. Thank you, Bradley, for giving him such a happy week."

"Bradley took care of me," said Timmy. "He played with me

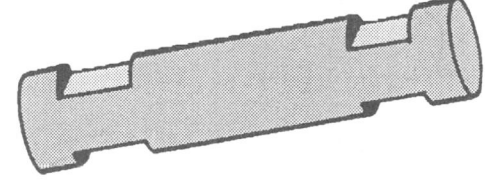

all the time when he got home from school. He let me play with all his tractors and trucks and everything."

Bradley's face got red, but he waved to Timmy as he drove away with his daddy.

As Bradley and Mother went into the house she said, "I think Timmy had a good time. Did you?"

"Not very," said Bradley.

"Why not? Did Timmy break some of your things?"

"No," said Bradley. "No, he didn't."

Mother waited a little, but Bradley didn't say anything else. So she said, "I must get my wash off the line."

"I must let Rocket out," said Bradley. But he was thinking, *I must get my Lincoln Logs out of the shed and back into my toy closet while Mother is at the wash line.*

Mother had taken only one dress off the line when she heard Bradley shout. Then around the house came Rocket. From his mouth flapped a torn piece of blue plastic.

"That looks like some of the plastic sheet Daddy put over the woodpile last winter," she said to herself.

"Rocket, you bad puppy! So that is what you did when you were penned in the shed this week!"

Rocket raced around the yard. He ran to Mother and jumped up on her. She pushed him down.

Then he dropped the torn plastic and began to chew on the wash basket.

Mother pushed him away again. Rocket ran off around the house.

Then Mother heard Bradley shout again. She picked up the piece of plastic. As she went around the house toward the shed, she heard Bradley yell, "Rocket, you get out of here!"

Then out from the shed ran the big puppy. This time he had something else in his mouth. It was brown.

Bradley came crying to the door of the shed. "Mother, come and look at what Rocket did! There's not one of them left!"

Mother ran into the shed. She could not believe what she saw on the floor. "Bradley! Your Lincoln Logs! They are all chewed up! How did they get out here?"

"Well, I . . ." and Bradley wiped his eyes on his sleeve.

Little by little the story came out.

Mother said, "Did you forget what Daddy told you about selfishness making you unhappy?"

"But I didn't know this would happen. If Timmy hadn't come . . ."

"Bradley, you were unhappy before you knew about these chewed-up logs. You were unhappy all week."

"But if Rocket hadn't . . ."

"Bradley, look at me," said Mother.

Bradley's face got as red as his eyes when he looked up.

"Who brought these logs out here?"

"I did."

"Why did you do that?"

"Because I was—"

"Because you were what?"

Bradley did not want to say the word, but Mother waited.

At last the word came out in a whisper. "Selfish."

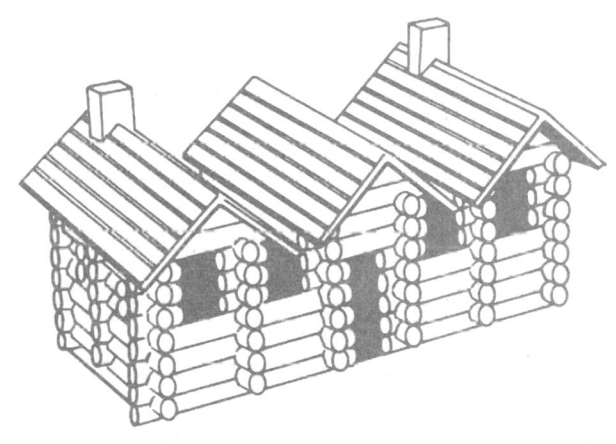

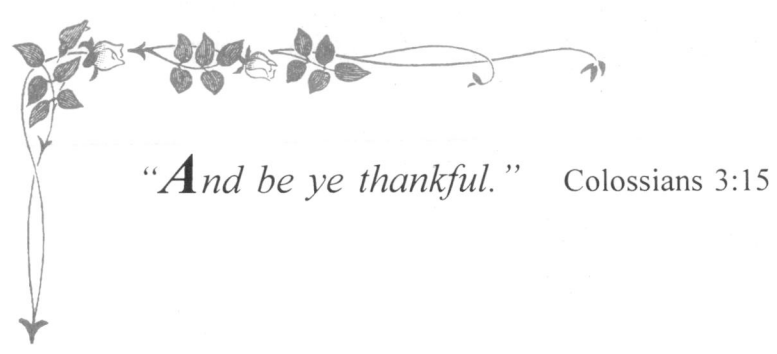

*"**A**nd be ye thankful."*   Colossians 3:15

Forgotten Thank You's

Why did Tommy forget his thank-you's?

"What was your Sunday school lesson about?" Father asked Tommy on the way home from church.

"We had the story of the ten **leopards** that Jesus **healed**."

"You mean **lepers**?"

"Oh, yes, lepers—those men who had that **awful** something on their skin.

They had to stay away from other people. They couldn't live in their own houses. They couldn't ever go home."

"Then what happened?"

"Jesus made them well. Their skin was all right again. And you know what? Only *one* of them said thank you to Jesus! The other nine went away without saying anything!"

"That wasn't very nice, was it?" said Mother. "But maybe they were so happy to be well that they just forgot."

"They should not have forgotten what Jesus had done," said Tommy. "Just think! They could go home now! They didn't have to stay away from other people.

"And the teacher said if you were a leopard—I mean leper—a doctor could not help you. You would just have to die! So Jesus really saved their lives.

"All but one forgot to say thank you. I would have been like that one, if I had been there. I would not have forgotten to say thank you."

"I hope you wouldn't have," said Father as they drove in the driveway.

"I am sure I wouldn't have," said Tommy. He hopped out of the car and ran up the walk to the house.

"M-m-m-m-m. I smell something good," he cried the next minute. "Smells like **roast** beef!"

Tommy ate lots of roast beef, **mashed potatoes**, and peas for dinner. He ate apple **sauce** and **chocolate** cake with chocolate icing.

When he left the table he said, "That

was a good dinner, Mother." But he didn't say anything else.

Tommy went out to play. Soon he called in the back door, "Mother, do you know where my ball and bat are?"

"I saw them behind the porch door," said Mother.

Tommy looked behind the porch door. "Yes, here they are! Good!" he cried. But he did not say anything else.

He took the bat and ball and ran out. Soon he was back. He was shaking his hand and almost crying. "Mother, I got a **splinter** in my hand. It hurts!"

Mother stopped washing dishes. She soon had the splinter out of Tommy's hand. She put some **fizzy** stuff on the place. Then she put a Band-Aid on it.

"That feels better," said Tommy with

a smile. But he did not say anything else.

When it was suppertime, Mother asked, "What do you want for supper?"

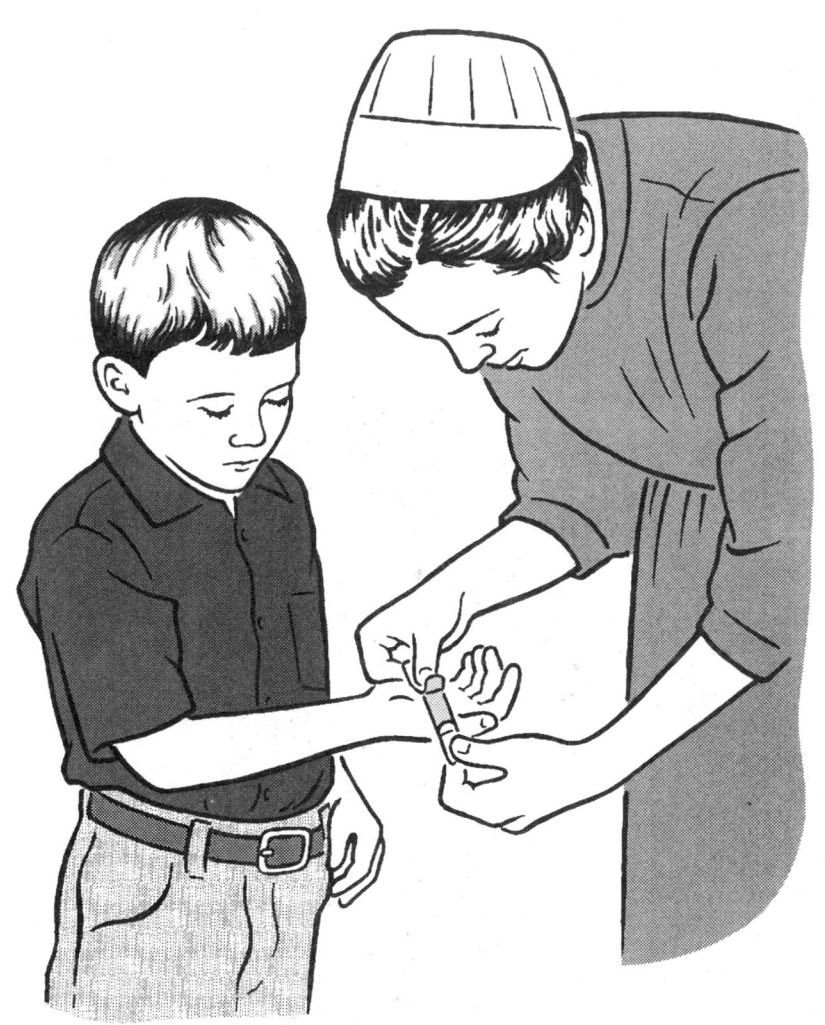

"Bacon-and-egg **sandwiches** and hot chocolate," cried Tommy.

"Thanks for the good idea. That is what I will make," said Mother. And she did.

At supper Tommy ate a bacon-and-egg sandwich. Then he ate half of another one. He drank a mug of hot chocolate. He ate a dish of peaches. He ate a piece of chocolate cake with chocolate icing.

He said, "I ate so much I cannot eat another bite." But he did not say anything else.

Even when Father said, "Thank you, dear, that was a good supper," Tommy didn't say anything.

That evening Tommy got ready for bed. He crawled up on the sofa beside Mother. "Please tell me a story. A story about a boy my size."

"All right," said Mother. And she began.

"Once there was a little boy who liked to go to Sunday school. One Sunday the Bible story was about the ten leopards."

"You *know* they weren't leopards, Mother," said Tommy with a laugh and a wiggle of joy. He liked stories about himself.

"Oh, weren't they leopards? Ten *lepers*, then," said Mother with a smile.

"Well, this little boy said it was awful that only one leper went back to thank Jesus for making him well. He said he was sure he would have gone back to say thank you. *He* would not have forgotten.

"Then this little boy ate a big dinner of roast beef and mashed potatoes and peas and apple sauce and chocolate cake with chocolate icing. He forgot to say thank you to his mother for making the good dinner.

"After a while he couldn't find his ball and bat. His mother told him where they were. The little boy was glad. But he forgot to say thank you to his mother for finding them.

"Pretty soon he came running in with a splinter in his hand. It really hurt. His mother pulled out the splinter. She put some fizzy stuff on it and a Band-Aid. The little boy said it felt a lot better. But he forgot to say thank you. He just ran out to play.

"At supper time the little boy's mother made bacon-and-egg sandwiches and hot chocolate because that is what the little boy said he wanted. He ate peaches. He also ate another piece of chocolate cake with chocolate icing.

"He ate so much he said he could not eat another bite. But he forgot to say thank you when he left the table."

Long before Mother had gotten to this part of the story, Tommy had stopped smiling. His head hung lower and lower.

When Mother stopped talking, he looked up at her and said, "I guess I forgot just as bad as the nine lepers, didn't I?"

"Yes, Tommy," said Mother. "You see, it is easy to forget to say thank you when we think only of how happy *we* are. We must get into the habit of thinking of what *others* have done for us. We must think of how hard they worked, or how much time they spent to help us. And we must think of what they might have given up to do something for us. Then we won't forget to say thank you."

Tommy crawled into his mother's lap and put his arms around her neck. "Thank you, thank you, thank you, thank you," he said. He gave her a kiss after each one.

"Now, I guess I'm caught up with my thank you's for today."

"No, there is one more you haven't said."

"There is?" he asked, thinking hard. "Oh, I know, now." Tommy slipped to his knees and closed his eyes. "Thank You, dear God, for the nice things You gave me today—the good things to eat, and my good mother, and the good stories in Sunday school. And help me not to forget to say thank you anymore after this. Amen."

Then Tommy was ready to hop into bed. The smile was back on his face.

Tommy's mother loved him and helped him see how he was not being thankful. Do you know of any other person who is just like your mother?

Only One Mother

Hundreds of stars in the pretty sky,
  Hundreds of shells on the shore together,
Hundreds of birds that go singing by,
  Hundreds of lambs in the sunny weather.

Hundreds of dewdrops to greet the dawn,
  Hundreds of bees in the purple clover,
Hundreds of butterflies on the lawn,
  But only one mother the wide world over.

–George Cooper

Just like Tommy, the child in this poem had something he liked for supper. Do you have something special you like to eat for supper?

Animal Crackers

Animal crackers, and cocoa to drink,

That is the finest of suppers, I think;

When I'm grown up and can have what
    I please

I think I shall always insist upon these.

What do *you* choose when you're
    offered a treat?

When Mother says, "What would you
    like best to eat?"

Is it waffles and syrup, or cinnamon
    toast?

It's cocoa and animals that *I* love most!

The kitchen's the coziest place that
    I know:
The kettle is singing, the stove is
    aglow,
And there in the twilight, how jolly
    to see
The cocoa and animals waiting for me.

Daddy and Mother dine later in state,
With Mary to cook for them, Susan
    to wait;
But they don't have nearly as much
    fun as I
Who eat in the kitchen with Nurse
    standing by;

And Daddy once said, he would like
    to be me
Having cocoa and animals once more
    for tea!

–Christopher Morley

"Look not every man on his own things, but every man also on the things of others." Philippians 2:4

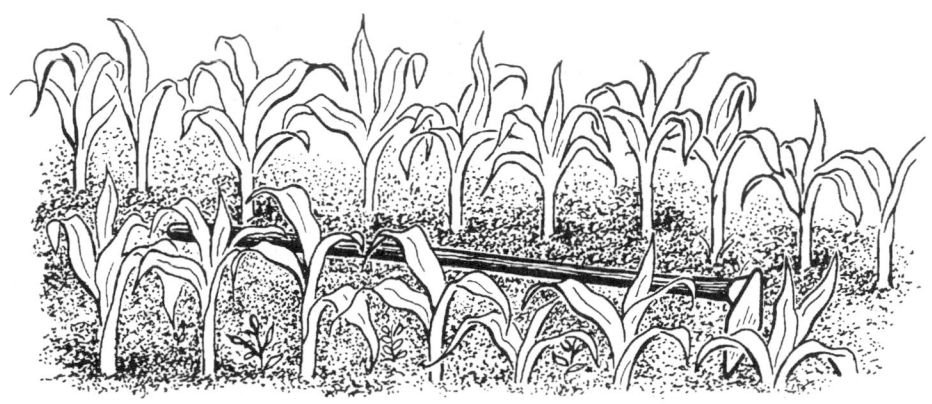

Long-Handled Hoe

A Story from Africa

Why did Kasala want to make a long-handled hoe when he would not use it himself?

"I must hoe the field," said Mother. "You come with me, Kasala. I need you to watch the baby."

I am getting too big to go to the field

with girls and women, thought Kasala. Then he said, "Mother, I am bigger than I was last summer. Soon I can go hunting with the men. I will not need to watch the baby when you hoe with the girls and women."

"Then who will watch him for me? We have no girls in our family to do that. I cannot work fast with the baby on my back."

Mother and Kasala went outside the village to the field. Baby brother was **tied** to Mother's back. His little fat feet **stuck** out on each side. His little black head **bobbed** along, **bobbity**-bobbity-bob.

On Mother's head was a basket with their lunch. The basket went bobbity-bobbity-bob, too. But it never fell off, no matter how much it bobbed.

Kasala had Mother's hoe. As he walked along he went **chop**, chop, chop at the weeds beside the path.

At the field, Mother set down the lunch basket. She put the baby on the grass. "Now watch him," she said. "You are a good help, Kasala. I can work so much faster when I do not have the baby on my back."

Mother took the hoe. She went down the corn row, chop, chop, chop. She had to **bend** way over because the **handle** of the hoe was just about two feet long. All the women in the village had hoes with short handles. All the women bent over as they worked. Kasala had never seen any other kind of hoe.

As Kasala watched his mother, he thought of something. His friend Jara had said, "One time the **hunters** went far over Three Mountains. They went to a village. There they saw women who worked in the fields. They had hoes with long handles. The women stood **straight** when they hoed. A teacher from far over the sea had **showed** them the strange new kind of hoe."

Kasala thought, *How fine it would be if Mother had a long-handled hoe. Then she could stand straight when she hoed. Then her back would not hurt at night.*

All at once he thought, *Maybe I could make her a long-handled hoe. I will ask Father to help. I will surprise her.*

That night he told Father about the long-handled hoe. "I want to make one for Mother," he said.

Father said, "My mother used a short-handled hoe. My grandmother used a short-handled hoe. No one in our tribe ever used a long-handled hoe. New ways are not always good. But a long-handled hoe might be good. I will see what we can do."

Kasala **slipped** into the mud hut and got the short-handled hoe. Mother was outside making supper over the fire.

Father and Kasala went to a place where Mother could not see them. Father took out the short handle. He made a new long one. He fit the new long handle into the hoe.

Kasala tried out the hoe that evening. It worked fine. He hid the hoe where Mother would not see it before morning. Would she like the new way of hoeing?

In the morning Mother said, "I must hoe the field again. Come with me, Kasala. I need you to watch the baby."

Kasala ran and got the new long-handled hoe. "Let's go," he said with a smile. He watched Mother's face.

Mother's eyes got big. She looked and looked at the hoe. "What do you have?

What have you done to my hoe?"

"Father and I have made it much better," Kasala said. "It is a new kind. You will not need to bend over with this one. Come, I will show you how it works."

Kasala could hardly wait to get to the field. He would show Mother how to use the new hoe. He would chop weeds without bending over.

Boys and men did not work in the fields. But just this once he would hoe to show Mother the new way.

At the field, he started down the row with the new hoe. Chop, chop, chop. The weeds fell **thick** and fast. Chop, chop, chop.

Other women and girls were coming to the field now. What did they see? A boy hoeing! He was not leaning over at all!

What did he have? Such a long-handled hoe! Where did it come from? What new way was this?

"This is a fine new way," laughed Kasala. "Mother, you sit and watch the baby. I shall hoe one row. A boy can use this new kind of hoe."

Kasala got to the end of the row before any of the women. "See, the new kind of hoe is better."

Mother could hardly wait to try out the long-handled hoe. Kasala gave it to her. Then he sat in the shade and watched. Chop, chop, chop. She did not bend over. She stood straight and tall as she chopped.

Her back will not hurt tonight, thought Kasala, with a smile. *New ways can be good.*

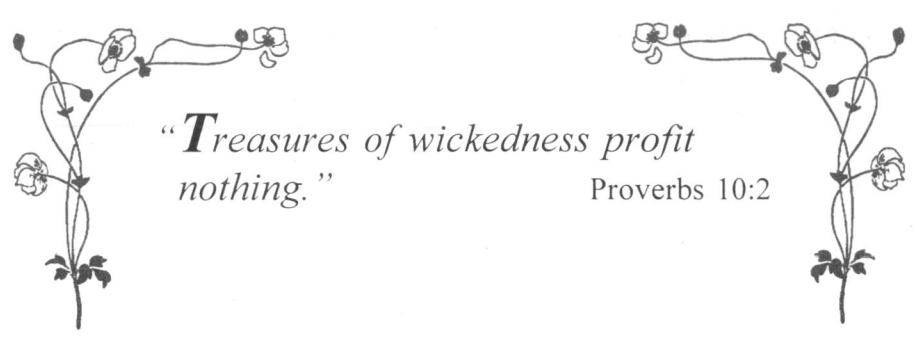

Tall for His Age

Part 1

What two classes were hard for Jay?

Jay was tall for his age. Mother said he took after Daddy.

His grandmother from out **West** said, "My! How Jay is growing!"

His aunt from the **East** said, "Jay-boy, I can't believe you are this tall and only seven years old!"

His uncle from up **North** said, "Jay has really shot up since I saw him last!"

His grandpa from down **South** said, "Taking after your daddy, aren't you? Going to be a beanpole like him, I reckon!"

Jay got a little tired of people talking about how tall he was for his age. He got tired of people asking what grade he was in. He could tell by their faces that they were surprised he was only in second grade. He knew they thought he should be in fourth or fifth.

Sometimes he would say, "I am seven years old," so they would know that he was in the right grade for his age.

Most of the time he liked being tall for his age.

He found out it was good to be tall in school. He got to help Miss Ramer when she needed someone to **reach** high places. He liked that.

He got to stand in the **middle** of the back row when they sang at the nursing home. He liked that, too.

And he liked having his desk in the back of the room. He could look over the heads of the other children. He could see all that was going on.

Jay found out that the other children wanted him on their side when they played kick ball. He could kick a ball farther than anyone else. He could run faster than anyone else because his legs were long.

He found out the other children wanted to be on his side when they played keep-away. He was tall enough to catch the ball over the heads of the other children.

Yes, he liked being tall in school.

But he found out that being tall for his age did not help in his schoolwork.

Many times he thought, *I may be the fastest runner, but I know I am the slowest reader. I wish I could read as fast as Lottie.*

*I may be the best at keep-away, but I am the **worst** at math. I wish I could add and take away as well as Eli does.*

Miss Ramer tried to help him. She said, "Just do your best, Jay. You do not need to read as fast as Lottie. You do not need to add and take away as well as Eli. Just do your best."

But Jay still **hated** to read out loud, because he read so slowly. He still hated to tell out loud how many he missed in math. He never got 100 like Eli did.

Then one day Jay found out something else he could do because he was tall for his age.

It was right before **recess**. He was sitting in his desk looking at his math worksheet. Math class was after recess. Jay did not have his worksheet done. He did not have even one answer written down. He could not remember what 15 take away 9 was.

That was when Jay found out that he was tall enough to look down on the desk in front of him.

Eli sat in front of him. Eli was working on his math too. He was going across the page writing the answers one right after the other. Jay could see all the answers.

He is on the third row, thought Jay. *And I am stuck on the first **problem**.*

I will never get my worksheet done before recess!

Jay looked at Miss Ramer.

She was writing at the blackboard.

Then he began to **copy** the answers from Eli's paper to his own. He wrote fast. He **copied** every answer in every row. He copied the answer to the last problem on his paper just after Eli wrote it down.

It was so easy! He couldn't believe it! His math was done in just about one minute! He was sure the answers would be right. Eli hardly ever missed any math problems.

Just then Eli turned around. Jay quickly slapped both hands on his paper.

"Don't you look at my paper," he whispered.

Eli turned back to his desk again. As Jay put his paper away, he felt his face getting red.

Why did I do such a silly thing? If Eli wanted to cheat, he would not try to copy my *paper! Anyway, my answers are the same as his. Why should I try to keep him from seeing them?*

Then he thought, *Eli does not need to cheat to get his answers right. I am the one who did that!*

Jay's thoughts went on and on. *I am the cheater, not Eli. I cheated only this one time, but now I am a cheater.*

God saw me, even if no one else did. What if the others find out!

"Cheater! Cheater! Cheater!" That is what they would say. They would not like him anymore. No one liked a cheater!

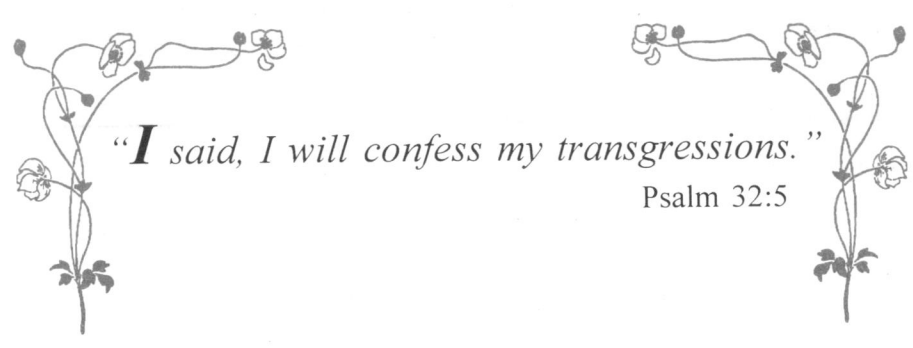

Tall for His Age

Part 2

What did Jay do that was harder than math?

What if Miss Ramer found out!
thought Jay. *Teachers never liked
cheaters. What would happen if she told
his mother and father?*

Suddenly Jay felt very lonely. He was
a cheater and no one liked him anymore.

Then he thought, *Only God knows*

what I did. I have not handed in my paper yet. I could erase Eli's answers and do the problems myself.

Jay got the worksheet from his desk. He took his pencil and tried to erase the answers.

It was not going to work. He rubbed as hard as he could, but he could still see the numbers he had first written. And it was almost recess time!

By this time Jay felt he would gladly do anything if he could get his own answers on his worksheet. What could he do now?

Well, he could pray. He shut his eyes, and in his heart he said, "Dear God, I am sorry I cheated. Please help me to know what to do now."

Right then he knew he would have to show his worksheet to Miss Ramer.

He would have to tell her he had copied
Eli's answers. He would have to ask her
how he could fix things right.

It was very hard for Jay to take his

paper to Miss Ramer and tell her all about it.

His teacher was very kind. She said, "I am glad you told me about this before math class.

"I will paste strips of paper over Eli's answers. Then you cannot see them. You can write your answers on the strips.

"You must stay in at recess to do them. Those you don't get done will just be wrong."

"I will be glad to do that," said Jay. And he really was.

Jay worked as fast as he could after the others went out to play. He didn't get the problems all done because they were take-aways. Take-aways were so much harder for him than adding problems.

But he was glad, glad, glad, that they were his own answers. He was not a cheater anymore!

When math class came, Miss Ramer said, "Today we will not trade papers. You may check your own."

Jay gave the teacher a thankful smile. She had done this for him. Now no one would see his sheet with the strips of paper pasted over Eli's answers.

Miss Ramer read the answers. She got out her grade book and said, "When I call your name, tell me how many you missed."

Jay had missed quite a few like he always did. But somehow he did not mind telling the number out loud this time. He smiled as he said it.

When the teacher called Eli's name, he began to laugh. "I missed them all,

Miss Ramer. I added them and they are all take-away problems. I just forgot to look at how we were to do them." He laughed again.

The other children laughed too.

All but Jay. He was looking at Miss Ramer with his eyes and mouth wide open.

Miss Ramer was looking at him, too. Then she smiled a big smile.

Then Jay, who was tall for his age, smiled a big, big smile back at her over the heads of all the other children.

"Every good gift and every perfect gift is from above." James 1:17

The I-Know Game

*What is your answer to the question
Daddy asked at the end of the story?*

Carrie and Andy were tired of standing at the **window**. They were tired of looking at the snow falling outside.

"Daddy, will you play the I-Know **guessing** game with us?" asked Andy.

"Please, Daddy," **begged** Carrie.

"All right," said Daddy. He shut his book. He put it on the desk.

"You can be the one who knows. Carrie and I will do the guessing," said Andy.

"All right. Let me think," said Daddy. "I know that today is **December** 31."

"But Daddy! Now you told us what it is! Now we can't guess!"

"That's right. I was just thinking out loud, I guess. That was not the I-Know game. Here it is. I know, **unless** God says no, that you two are going to get a **gift** tonight."

"A gift!" cried Andy, **hopping** first on one foot and then the other.

"Tonight!" cried Carrie.

Then they began asking questions to

212

help them guess what Daddy was thinking of.

"Is it big?" asked Carrie.

"Yes, it really is big," answered Daddy.

"How big? As big as my bicycle?" asked Andy.

"Well-l-l-l," said Daddy. "It is hard to say what size it is. It would be better to count it."

"Count it? Then it is more than one. Will we each get one?"

"No, it is only one thing, but it has many **parts**," said Daddy.

"Can I take it **apart**?" asked Andy.

"No, you can't take it apart."

"Can we play with it?" asked Carrie.

"No, it is not a toy, but you can use it," answered Daddy.

213

"What is it?" said Andy. "Have we ever seen one?"

"Well, I guess you can't really see it."

"But Daddy, how can we get a gift and use it if we can't see it?" cried Carrie.

Daddy laughed. "Your questions are too hard. That is the best answer I can give to that one."

"Does it have feet?" Andy asked. Maybe they would be getting the puppy they had been begging for.

"No feet," answered Daddy. "But it goes along pretty fast without feet."

Suddenly Andy asked, "Who is going to give it to us? Is it you? Is it Mother?"

"No, Mother and I could not give you one of these things."

"Then it must be God," guessed Carrie.

"Yes, it is God," said Daddy.

"How is He going to give it to us? Will He drop it down out of heaven?"

Daddy laughed again. "You two are asking me questions that I can hardly answer. No, I can't say that God will drop it out of heaven."

"Who will bring it then?"

"No one. It will—it will just sort of come. It will just sort of be here."

"Oh, Daddy! I give up," cried Carrie.

"So do I," said Andy. "Tell us what it is."

"Well, let me give you one more **hint**. Tonight, right after **midnight** you will start to have it."

Carrie and Andy looked at each other.

They were thinking hard.

"Tonight?" said Carrie slowly.

"Right after midnight?" said Andy slowly.

Then Carrie cried, "I know. I know what it is!"

And Andy cried, "So do I. It is the new **year**. We will get a new year!"

"Yes, you are right," said Daddy.

"A new year!" said Carrie. "But Daddy, we get one of them every year."

"A new year!" said Andy. "Is that a gift?"

Daddy smiled. "Well, is it?" he asked.

In the story, Carrie and Andy learned about a gift that they could not see. Here is a poem about something else no one can see. Do you think this is a gift? Can you think of a way the wind helps us?

The Wind

Who has seen the wind?
　Neither I nor you.
But when the leaves hang trembling,
　The wind is passing through.

Who has seen the wind?
　Neither you nor I.
But when the trees bow down their
heads,
　The wind is passing by.

—Christina Rossetti

The snow in this poem came as quietly in the middle of the night as the new year began for Carrie and Andy. After a deep drifting snow, it is a mystery what is under some of the strange shapes we see.

The Snow

Last night when we were sound asleep,
The snow fell fast, the snow piled deep.
When morning came and we looked out,
The snow was lying all about.

The wind was blowing high and low,
And wrinkling up the pure white snow;
And everywhere that we could see,
We found that God made mystery.

–Marguerite C. Clark

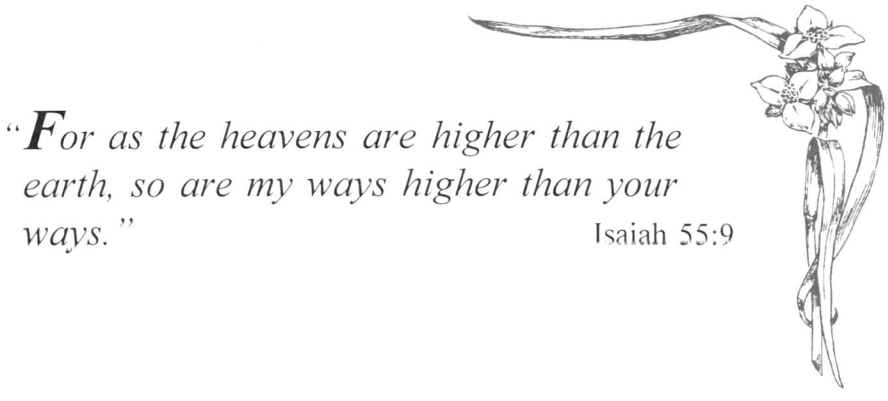

*"**F**or as the heavens are higher than the earth, so are my ways higher than your ways."*

Isaiah 55:9

The Wisdom of the Lord

Why did Hoja change his mind about where watermelons should grow?

In the days of old, there was a man called Hoja who had a big garden.

One **fair** day he went out to his garden to work. "God is good to me," said Hoja, as he looked around. "See how **everything** grows! I have **much** to give thanks for, with a garden as fair as this."

There was much to do in the garden. Hoja was **happy** as he worked.

After a time he wanted something to eat.

"I think I would like some watermelon," said he. He went to the watermelon **vines** to see if any were **ripe**. He looked until he found one that looked ripe. It was big, but not too big. It was just big enough.

As he started to pull it off the vine, he smiled. "Just think!" he said to himself. "This watermelon is two times as big as my head. Yet it does not grow on a big tree, as one would suppose. It grows on a **thin** little vine, not even as big as a **stick**! Now that is something to think about."

In the garden there was a cool, grassy place under a nut tree. Hoja liked to eat his lunch there. He went there with the watermelon.

As he was eating, he looked up at the tree. "I suppose God in his **wisdom**

knows what is best," he said. "But how can this be right? He makes little nuts grow on big trees and big watermelons grow on thin little vines. I would have done it just the other way around, if I were God."

Just then a nut **dropped** down through the leaves, down, down. It **landed** right on Hoja's head.

The nut surprised Hoja, but it did not hurt him, of course.

All at once he started to laugh. "In truth, O **Lord**," he said. "Now I see how little I know! What if this watermelon grew on this tree and had come down and landed on my head. That would not be a thing to laugh at.

"You who know everything, have put things where they should be—nuts, watermelons, and all."

Here is a poem that shows the greatness of the Lord. It tells of something big and beautiful God made. We can see it, but we cannot feel it or smell it. We cannot hear or taste or use it. We can only look at it and enjoy it and thank God for another beautiful thing He made.

The Rainbow

Boats sail on the rivers,
And ships sail on the seas;
But clouds that sail across the sky
Are prettier far than these.
There are bridges on the rivers,
As pretty as you please;
But God's bow that arches heaven,
And overtops the trees,
And builds a road from earth to sky,
Is prettier far than these.

–Christina Rossetti

The nut falling on Hoja's head made him glad that God in His wisdom made watermelons grow on the ground.

This poem tells of something else that shows God's wisdom. He made seeds so they need two things before they will grow. Read the poem and find what those two things are. Can you think why a seed must have both of them?

The Little Plant

In the heart of a seed,
    Buried deep, so deep,
A dear little plant
    Lay fast asleep!

"Wake!" said the sunshine,
    "And creep to the light."
"Wake!" said the voice
    Of the raindrops bright.

The little plant heard
    And it rose to see
What the wonderful
    Outside world might be.

                    –Kate L. Brown

Have you ever sat so quietly that a bird did not know you were watching it? What do you call the kind of worms a robin eats?

A Bird

A bird came down the walk;
He did not know I saw;
He bit an angle-worm in halves
And ate the fellow, raw.

And then he drank a dew
From a convenient grass,
And then hopped sidewise
   to the wall
To let a beetle pass.

                    –Emily Dickinson

Flowers, birds, brooks, trees—can you see any of these from where you are right now? Whatever we see of God's creation should make us think of the One we cannot see, the One who loves us best of all.

Best of All

I love the sweet wildflowers that
    bloom
  Within the woodland way;
I love the little birds that sing
  And carol at their play.

I love the brook—the babbling
    brook,
  The trees so strong and tall.
But my dear Lord, who loveth me—
  I love Him best of all.

—Unknown

A Book!
In Our House!
That I Can Read!

Part 1

What Bible story was the teacher telling?

In a small house in a faraway land there was not one book. Shama lived there with her grandmother and grandfather. She was eight years old and had no book. She could not even read.

Grandfather could read, but not many others in the village could.

"I wish I could read," Shama said. "I wish I had a book. I wish I could read the words we talk with."

Grandmother said, "Whoever heard of a girl reading? What I know, I have learned by living many years. If you want to know **anything**, ask me. I can tell you all you need to know."

Grandfather said, "Yes, why should a girl know how to read? It would not help her keep the house clean. It would not help her carry water from the well. It would not help her bring my halva from the sweet shop."

Grandfather was glad he could read. But he saw no need for a girl to learn to read.

So Shama did not learn to read.

She did not see how she ever could have a book of her own.

Instead, she helped Grandmother work in the little house. She **swept** the floor. She carried water. She put the beds into the sun to air out. And she went to **market** with Grandmother.

Every day she went to the sweet shop to buy halva. Grandfather liked to eat it with his dinner.

Shama worked hard, but there was time every day to play with her best friend Jameela.

One day as they played with their balls in the yard, Shama heard a bell. *Tin–tun, tin–tun, tin–tun, tin–tun.*

The bell was ringing on the far side of a wheat field.

"I **wonder** who is ringing that bell.

Why would they be ringing a bell?" she asked.

"I don't know," said Jameela.

The bell began again. *Tin–tun, tin–tun, tin–tun.*

"Let's go and see where it is coming from." Shama began to run. Jameela ran after her.

They ran along the village street. They ran along the path to the wheat field. They ran around the wheat field to the other side.

At last they stopped. They had come to a high **bamboo** fence. Once more they heard the bell. It rang on the other side of the fence. *Tin–tun, tin–tun, tin–tun.*

Then they heard a woman's voice. Had that woman **rung** the bell? Why

would she ring a bell?

The bamboo fence was very high. The girls could not see over it. They could hear the woman's voice. She **seemed** to be telling a story. She must be a **teacher**.

Maybe she could teach me to read, thought Shama.

Shama and Jameela peeped through **cracks** in the bamboo fence. They saw a lady. She was sitting on a low **stool**. She had a black book in her hands. Village children sat on the ground in front of her.

This must be a school, thought Shama. *She has a book. She can read!*

The teacher was saying, "Then a Samaritan, as he was going along the road, saw the poor hurt man. He went to him and **fixed** his hurt places."

"Let's go in," whispered Shama. "There must be a gate somewhere."

Jameela nodded.

The girls ran along the bamboo fence until they came to an open gate. Soon they were sitting on the ground with the other children.

The teacher smiled at them. She went on with the story. "When the Samaritan went on his way, he said to the keeper of the inn, 'Take good care of him. If you spend any more money, I will pay you when I come back this way.'"

That was the end of the story. Some of the children began to talk. One said, "Now the poor man is safe!"

Another said, "I'm glad the Samaritan came along. Those others just left him to die."

The teacher said, "The Samaritan did not know the hurt man. He helped him out of the goodness of his heart. That is the way we should be, too.

"I have many more stories in this book. This book is the Bible. It tells about God, who made our world. He loves everyone. Tomorrow when you hear the bell, come again. I will tell you another story."

Shama and Jameela walked home talking. "I wish we had not missed the first part of the story," said Jameela. "I wish I knew how the poor man got hurt."

"I wish we knew about those others who left him to die," put in Shama. "Why would anyone do that? We missed the in-between part too, while we were looking for the gate. If we could read, the teacher might let us read the story from her book. Then we could find out why that man was lying along the road half dead."

"Let's come tomorrow," said Jameela.

"Yes, let's. Stop for me when you hear the bell," said Shama. "Let's ask if she is going to teach children to read."

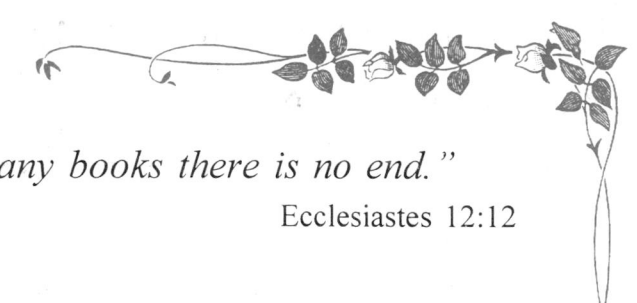

"Of making many books there is no end."

Ecclesiastes 12:12

A Book!
In Our House!
That I Can Read!

Part 2

*What did Grandfather think about the Bible
at the end of the story?*

Shama told Grandmother and
Grandfather all that she and Jameela
had seen and heard.

Grandfather said, "The Bible is the

book of the Christians. I do not know
what kind of teaching is in the Bible.
Our people do not believe that way.
Do not go there again."

"But Grandfather!" cried Shama,
"the teacher might teach me to read.
Then I could read the Bible. I could find
out if it is a good book or not."

"Our ways are good enough for
Grandmother and me. They are good
enough for you too. Say no more about
it."

The next day Jameela stopped by.
"Come, Shama, the bell is ringing. It is
time to go."

Shama shook her head. "I cannot go.
Grandfather says no."

"You must beg him," said Jameela.
"At first my father said I could not go.
Then I begged and begged. I started

to cry. Then he said I could go."

Shama shook her head again. "That would not work with Grandfather."

So Jamecla ran off to the school behind the bamboo fence. Shama went sadly to the sweet shop to buy halva for Grandfather.

This time the shopkeeper did not wrap the halva in a wide green leaf. He wrapped it in a sheet of paper. The paper had some strange little black marks on it.

Shama knew the black marks were words. Oh, if she could only read what the words said!

"Look, Grandfather," she cried as soon as she got home. "The shopkeeper wrapped the halva in this paper. See the words! Read them! Read them!"

Grandfather took the paper off the halva. As he ate, he looked at the words on the paper. He read them over and over.

Then he said, "These words say a strange thing: 'You shall love your neighbor as yourself.' How could anyone do that? Only if you had much love in your heart, could you do that. It would be a wonderful thing if everyone loved his neighbor as much as he loved himself."

Then he said to Shama, "Tomorrow ask the shopkeeper to wrap my halva in another sheet of this paper."

When Shama came home the next day, Grandfather took the new sheet of paper. He sat down and read it over and over. He said, "This paper has words that say something else strange. It says,

'If any one would be first, he must be last and servant of all.'

"How strange! Whoever thought of such a thing? Being first because you are last? Being first because you are a servant? How could a servant be first?

"It would be wonderful if everyone would be willing to be last instead of trying to be first. It would be wonderful if everyone would be willing to be a servant."

Suddenly Grandfather got up. "Come, Shama, we will go to the sweet shop. We will see if the shopkeeper has more of these papers. The words on these papers are strange; but they tell of good ways for people to treat each other."

At the sweet shop, Grandfather asked the shopkeeper about the papers with words on them.

"Yes, I have some left. A man sold them to me cheap. It is good paper to wrap things in. I cannot read the words. I think they come from an old book."

Grandfather paid the shopkeeper for all the papers he had left.

At home he sat down and began to read. Shama watched him turn the pages. She wished and wished she could read those little black marks. She wanted to know what they said.

"It is a story," Grandfather said at last. "It tells about a man who was going along a lonely road. Some robbers jumped out and took all his things. They beat him and ran away. The poor man was half-dead.

"A priest came along. He saw the man but he went by on the other side.

"Then a Levite came along. He went and looked at the half-dead man. But he, too, went on.

"Then a Samaritan came along. He saw the half-dead man. He went and looked at him and . . . that is the end of the page. It is the last page. Now we don't know what the Samaritan did!"

"Oh, Grandfather!" Shama cried, "I know! I know! That is the same story the teacher told! Now I know the first part!

"The Samaritan helped the half-dead man. He took him to an inn. He paid to have him taken care of. He was so kind to the hurt man. The man wasn't anyone he knew. The Samaritan helped him out of the goodness of his heart. And the teacher said that's the way we should be."

Grandfather said, "These pages must be from the Christians' book. They must be part of their Bible. All I have read tells of good ways to live. It would be good for our people to know about these ways."

Then he said to Shama, "Tomorrow when the bell rings, you may go to that school. Tell the teacher you want to hear more stories. I see that the things in the Christian book are good, even for a girl to know.

"Someday maybe we can have all of this Christian book. Then it would be good for you to know how to read it. You may ask the teacher about it."

"A book! In our house! That I can read!" Shama said these words over and over as she ran to tell Jameela.

"Now therefore be ye not mockers."   Isaiah 28:22

A Story Full
of Pockets

Who was the mocker in this story?

Janie went **hippety**-hop and
skippety-skip all the way to school. She
was too happy to walk. It was a pretty
day. She liked school and she was
wearing her dress with the deep, deep
pocket on the right side.

Janie **caught** up with Nan who was
walking to school too.

"Hi, Nan," she said. "Look at my
deep, deep pocket."

"I have two pockets," said Nan, showing them to Janie.

"But they are *teeny, tiny* pockets. Mine is *deep, deep*."

"Huh!" said a boy's voice. "Girls don't have as many pockets as boys do."

The girls looked up and saw Mark standing by the walk.

"See," he said. "I have two in the front of my pants and two in the back. Then I have two in my sweater—that makes six."

"Six!" laughed another voice. Janie turned and saw Bucky Brown standing near the steps. Bucky was a poor boy. He always tried to act **tough**. His clothes were torn and dirty.

Bucky began to count his pockets. "One, two, three, four, five, and a pencil pocket. I have a watch pocket in my **overalls**. And four in my **jacket**. That makes **eleven** in all." He smiled in a friendly way. He looked nice when he smiled.

"Look out, or you will count some of those holes in your overalls for pockets," said Mark with a laugh that was not very friendly.

Janie looked at Bucky. His smile was gone. The tough look was back on his face. He did not look nice now.

He made fists and took a step toward Mark. "That will be enough out of you," he growled, "unless you want some holes in that sissy sweater of yours."

Janie said quickly, "I have something in my pocket."

"So have I," said Nan. "See, I have a **quarter** for my lunch. I have a roll of

mints to eat at recess, and a white **hanky**."

"Girls don't carry much in their pockets," said Mark. "Look at what I have in mine."

He took out a quarter for his lunch, some rubber bands, a pad of paper, a pencil, a hanky, and a candy bar for recess.

"Is that all you have?" asked Bucky. He was smiling again. "Look at what I have."

He began to **empty** his eleven pockets. He had two stubby pencils, some rubber bands, a **squirt** gun, scrap paper, **bubble** gum that had been chewed, some pretty black-and-white stones, a butterfly wing, a watch with no hands, and some nails. No candy, no hanky, no quarter for lunch.

"Bucky," cried Janie. "You need all your pockets to carry your things. What a lot of interesting things you have."

"Junk," said Mark, making a face. "Just plain junk. That's all it is."

Janie saw the smile leave Bucky's face again. The tough look came back. Again he made fists and started toward Mark. Mark backed away.

"Oh, Bucky, you haven't seen what I have in my pocket yet." Janie reached into her deep, deep pocket and pulled out a picture.

"Just a picture," began Bucky. Then he stopped. It was a picture of Jesus blessing the children. He was holding a little child on His lap. He had His arm around another child. Many other children stood close to Him. They were looking up into His face.

Under the picture were the words, "Let the children come to me."

The tough look went out of Bucky's eyes. "That's a nice picture. It's Jesus, isn't it?"

Then Janie thought, *I don't think Bucky is tough inside. He just acts that way because other children tease him.*

Then Bucky said, "Janie, what'll you take for that picture? You can have anything I've got."

"No, Bucky," she said, "I wouldn't want to take any of your things. But you can have the picture for nothing. I have another one like it at home."

Just then the first bell rang. Bucky began picking up his things and stuffing them into his pockets.

But Janie saw that he saved one

pocket in his jacket for the picture of
Jesus. He slid it in very carefully and
snapped the flap shut.

He smiled happily, and they all went
into the schoolhouse together.

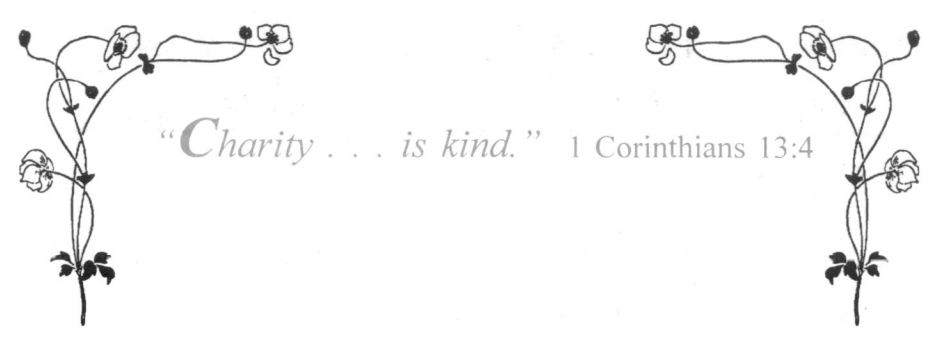

Too Big and Too Little

What put the smile on Freddie's face?

Tilly was getting ready for **company**. Her friend Ann was coming over soon. They were going to play house.

Tilly took her little table out on the side porch. She took out her chairs. She got her toy bear and puppy and put them at the table. Now all she **needed** were her doll bed and dolls.

"Tilly, may I please ride your bike?"

Tilly looked around. There stood Freddie. He lived next door.

She looked at her new bike. She had put it under the tree so Ann could see it.

They were not going to ride the bike. She just wanted Ann to see it. But she

didn't want Freddie to ride it.

"I guess not," she said. "Ann is coming over pretty soon to play with me."

"Were you going to ride your bike?" asked Freddie.

"No, we are going to play house," said Tilly.

"Well, then, why can't I ride the bike?"

"Because," said Tilly.

"Because why?" asked Freddie.

"Because—because—because you are too big. And it's a girl's bike."

Tilly **knew** that didn't sound like a very good reason. But she just didn't want Freddie riding her bike.

Freddie looked sadly at her. Then he looked sadly at her bike under the tree.

He didn't say anything more. He just turned and walked back toward his home.

Tilly went on with her work. She brought out her dolls and the doll bed. She began to sweep the porch.

She could still see Freddie. He was down at the **sidewalk** looking up the street. He looked **lonely**.

Then three boys came into sight. They had a big ball. They were **tossing** the ball back and **forth** between them as they walked along.

As they came close, she heard Freddie ask, "May I play too?"

But the boys walked on, tossing the ball back and forth. One of the boys said, "Sorry, Freddie, you are too little for this game."

Tilly stopped sweeping. She looked over at Freddie. He was standing there looking after the boys. Now he looked more lonely than ever.

Tilly was thinking, *I told him he was too big, and those boys told him he was too little. He can't help what size he is.*

Suddenly she called. "Freddie, come over here a minute."

Freddie came slowly across the yard.

"What do you want?" he asked. He looked about ready to cry.

Tilly smiled at him. "I **changed** my mind, Freddie. When Ann comes, we are going to need someone to be our helper boy. We will need a boy big enough to go to the store and get our groceries. He will have to go on the bike. Would you be our boy?"

259

"Oh, yes," cried Freddie. He didn't look sad. He didn't look lonely now.

"Give me time to make out my list." Tilly got a **piece** of **paper**. She pretended to write.

"Here is the list. Do you think you can get all of that on the back of your pickup?"

Freddie took the paper. He pretended to read the list. He **nodded** his head. "I can get all of those things."

He put the paper into his pocket and got on the bike. "I'll drive carefully," he said with a happy smile.

Tilly watched him ride down the sidewalk. There was a happy smile on her face, too. Freddie was not too big. He was not too little, either. He was just right the way he was.

Study Words

Study words in the reader, and the page number for each.

A

ahead, 112
alone, 51
along, 52
answer, 12
anything, 229
apart, 213
aren't, 119
arm, 99
arrow, 88
awful, 174

B

bamboo, 231
bark, 23
basket, 112
beautiful, 2
begged, 210
bend, 190
between, 42
bleed, 120
bobbed, 189
bobbity, 189
bones, 27
born, 28
bother, 90
bottom, 58
bow, 88
brave, 54
broken, 97
bubble, 250
bunk, 58
butterfly, 136

C

cabin, 19
calendar, 30
captain, 147

carefully, 112
carried, 41
carry, 41
caterpillar, 128
caught, 246
cellar, 4
certificate, 29
chair, 43
changed, 258
cheerful, 81
chewed, 161
chocolate, 176
chop, 190
chrysalis, 134
clouds, 63
coasting, 114
coax, 24
company, 254
complained, 81
cookies, 40
copied, 202
copy, 202
corn, 87
couldn't, 40
country, 30
cousin, 158
covered, 21
cracks, 233
crossly, 80
crying, 106
cupboard, 42

D

December, 211
deck, 148
delivery, 114
didn't, 256
died, 157

dinnertime, 73
doesn't, 119
doorstep, 112
dried, 2
drive, 146
dropped, 222
drove, 50
dumped, 97

E

east, 196
easy, 102
edge, 31
eight, 28
eleven, 248
empty, 250
enjoy, 121
everything, 219

F

fact, 118
fair, 219
fault, 109
fellow, 108
fifteen, 110
fishing, 80
fixed, 233
fizzy, 177
flag, 149
flower, 4
forest, 88
forth, 257
friendly, 88

G

gift, 211
glumly, 119
grabbed, 112

264

Study Words for Each Story

Nell's Dried Onions

beautiful
dried
onions
throw
pantry
write
thank
think
flower
cellar
water
hyacinths

Johnny and the Blue Marble

verse
thou
seest
mean
wrong
should
speak
listen
marbles
answer
shoulder
school

Abe and His Dog

cabin
squirrels
leave
wagon
covered
strong
oxen
heavy

rivers
shiver
bark
coax

The Bag of Birthday Bones, Parts 1 and 2

bones
schoolroom
seven
eight
born
certificate
calendar
country
world
months
edge
spring

Mr. Doodleburger Comes to Work

cookies
couldn't
Mr.
carry
carried
squeezed
woodbox
Ma'am
between
cupboard
chair
picked

Emmy and the Big Black Dog

milk can
drove

alone
penned
yard
leap
pound
puffing
along
handed
mouse
brave

Story in a Story

staying
bunk
spare
slept
bottom
rumble
pitter
pour
scared
thump
clouds
milkweeds

The Apple That Was Polished Six Times

thought
polished
shirt
dinnertime
tired
present
lovely
rocked
groceries
whistled
nurse
sweater

265

The Cross Box

crossly
fishing
windmill
grumbled
complained
sobbed
grouchy
cheerful
slot
neither
hospital
pitch

An Indian's Gift

corn
Indian
friendly
taught
shoot
bow
arrow
handful
forest
wondered
grow
bother

Good-bye, Little Blue Jeep

vehicles
dumped
jeeps
broken
thirty
haven't
through
arm
hidden
truth
easy
hardest

Why Henry Was Late

record
crying
fellow
milkman
moments
whole
fault
hadn't
perhaps
size
fifteen
reason

Helping Hands

hurried
snowy
playmates
grabbed
ahead
basket
carefully
resting
doorstep
people
coasting
delivery

It Is Up to You

slide
himself
steps
fact
glumly
aren't
never
doesn't
slowpokes
skinned
bleed
enjoy

Baby Insect

caterpillar
stripes
watch
holes
plant
questions
insect
chrysalis
stages
wrinkled
butterfly
monarch

Captain or Deck Hand?

rail
stacked
pile
drive
stakes
pretend
captain
steers
deck
wheel
flag
telescope

Lesson of the Lincoln Logs, Parts 1 and 2

lesson
died
until
cousin
wasn't
spoil
load
plastic
shelf
rough

chewed
sheet

Forgotten Thank-You's

leopards
healed
lepers
awful
roast
mashed
potatoes
sauce
chocolate
splinter
fizzy
sandwiches

Long-Handled Hoe

tied
stuck
bobbed
bobbity
chop
bend
handle
hunters
straight
showed
slipped
thick

Tall for His Age, Parts 1 and 2

west
east
north
south
reach
middle

worst
hated
recess
problem
copy
copied

The I-Know Game

window
guessing
begged
December
unless
gift
hopping
parts
apart
hint
midnight
year

The Wisdom of the Lord

fair
everything
much
happy
vines
ripe
thin
stick
wisdom
dropped
landed
Lord

A Book! In Our House! That I Can Read! Parts 1 and 2

anything
instead

swept
market
wonder
bamboo
rung
seemed
teacher
cracks
stool
fixed

Story Full of Pockets

hippety
skippety
caught
tough
overalls
jacket
eleven
quarter
hanky
empty
squirt
bubble

Too Big and Too Little

company
needed
didn't
knew
sidewalk
lonely
tossing
forth
changed
piece
paper
nodded

267

Acknowledgements

"A Bird," by Emily Dickinson.

"A Book! In Our House! That I Can Read!" Adapted from HERE AND THERE WITH THE BIBLE by Elizabeth Allstrom. Copyright 1960 by Friendship Press, Inc.

"A Cricket," by Aileen Fisher, from CRICKET IN A THICKET Scribner's, NY, 1963. Used by permission of the author.

"A Story Full of Pockets." Adapted from "Story Full of Pockets," by Lois Grieser Kauffman, BEAMS OF LIGHT, September, 1956. Mennonite Publishing House, Scottdale, PA. Used by permission.

"Abe and His Dog." Adapted from "Lincoln and His Dog," by Edna Riddleburger.

"All Things Bright and Beautiful," by Cecil F. Alexander.

"An Indian's Gift." Adapted fron "An Indian's Gift," NEW FRIENDS, The New Silent Readers, Book 2. ©1937 John C. Winston Company.

"Animal Crackers," by Christopher Morley.

"Baby Insect," by Ruth K. Hobbs, ©1998 Christian Light Publications, Inc. Harrisonburg, VA. All rights reserved

"Best of All." Author unknown.

"Captain or Deck Hand." Adapted from "I Want To Be the Captain," by Rebecca Martin, from STORY MATES. ©1992 Christian Light Publications, Inc.

"Coasting." Adapted from "Coasting," McGUFFEY'S SECOND ECLECTIC READER, American Book Company, New York, 1920.

"Cross Box," from THE HOWE READERS, Book 2.

"Emmy and the Big Black Dog," by Ruth K. Hobbs. ©1998 Christian Light Publications, Inc., Harrisonburg, VA. All rights reserved.

"Forgotten Thank You's." Adapted from "When Tommy Forgot," by Lois Kauffman. ©1958 Lois Kauffman. Used by permission.

"Four Seasons." From JACK AND JILL, copyright ©1946 by Curtis Publishing Company. Used by permission of Children's Better Health Institute, Benjamin Franklin Literary & Medical Society, Inc., Indianapolis, Indiana.

"Funny the Way Different Cars Start," by Dorothy W. Baruch, from I LIKE MACHINERY, published by Harper & Brothers.

"Fuzzy Wuzzy Creepy Crawly," by Lillian Schultze.

"Goodbye, Little Blue Jeep." Adapted from "Goodby, Little Soldier," OPEN DOORS, Second Reader. ©1957 American Book Company, New York, NY.

"Helping Hands." Adapted from "Helping Hands," Author Unknown, CHILDREN'S SECOND READER. Ginn and Company, New York, 1894.

"I'd Like to Be Worm," from JINGLE JANGLE by Zhenya Gay. Copyright ©1953 by Zhenya Gay. Copyright © renewed 1981 by Erika Hinchey. Used by permission of Viking Penguin, a division of Penguin Books USA, Inc.

"It Is up to You." Adapted from "Billy Proves His Friendliness," by Mabel Niedermeyer, BEAMS OF LIGHT, December, 1956. Mennonite Publishing House, Scottdale, PA. Used by permission.

"Johnny and the Blue Marble." Adapted from "Johnny and the Blue Marble," ANALYTICAL SECOND READER.